MW00680979

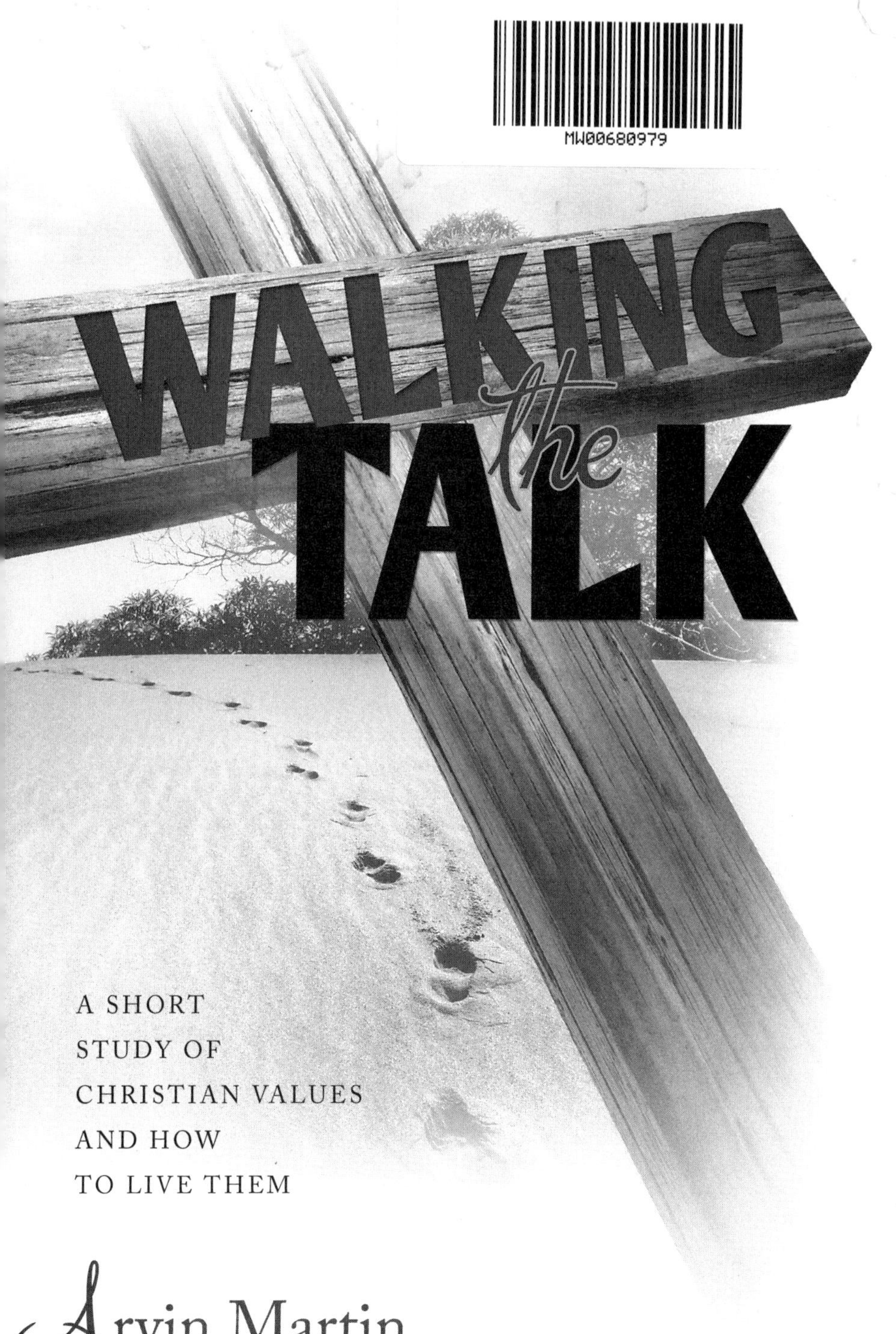

WALKING the TALK

A SHORT STUDY OF CHRISTIAN VALUES AND HOW TO LIVE THEM

Arvin Martin

WALKING THE TALK

Copyright © 2014 Vision Publishers
All rights reserved. For permission to quote from this book, contact Vision Publishers.
No permission is needed for 50 words or less

ISBN-10: 1-932676-90-2
ISBN-13: 978-1-932676-90-7

Also available as E-book:
ePUB-10: 1-932676-98-8
ePUB-13: 978-1-932676-98-3
ePDF-10: 1-932676-99-6
ePDF-13: 978-1-932676-99-0

Printed in the United States of America

Cover Design: Lanette Steiner
Text Layout & Design: Naomi Yoder

Scriptures are taken from the King James Version unless indicated otherwise.
Scripture taken from the New King James Version®. Copyright © 1982 by Thomas Nelson, Inc. Used by permission. All rights reserved.

For special discounts on bulk purchases, please contact:
Vision Publishers Orders by phone: 877.488.0901

For Information or Comments, Please Contact:
Vision Publishers
P.O. Box 190
Harrisonburg, VA 22803
Phone: 877.488.0901
Fax: 540.437.1969
E-mail: orders@vision-publishers.com
www.vision-publishers.com
(See order form in back)

Holmes Printing Solutions
8757 County Road 77 • Fredericksburg, Ohio 44627
888.473.6870

TABLE OF CONTENTS

INTRODUCTION

Western culture has created confusion in knowing right from wrong. Political battles have raged in legislatures and courts in an attempt to force people to make moral decisions. Some legislators, judges, and lobbyists do not walk the talk of the noble decrees they have helped to establish. Some well-known pastors have disappointed their listeners by violating the Bible commands they have proclaimed. In doing so, they have not walked what they have talked. Adding to the confusion, many Christian denominations have divided over disagreements about applications of Bible teaching. So then, what should guide our beliefs and our moral values? Should popular opinion, the legislatures, or judicial systems form the basis of our practices?

In quoting many Scriptures and explaining them, Martin shows that God retains the authority to be our spiritual Guide. It is one thing to be interested in the Scriptures and talk highly of them, but quite another to take the commands of Scripture literally in applying them to our daily walk of life. Martin promotes the concept that the one who is pleasing to God is a radical Biblicist. A Christian who is a radical Biblicist believes that in the Bible God defines right from wrong, and makes his moral and spiritual decisions accordingly. They say it is not enough to promote Biblical principles of faith, holiness, and love. We also need to walk the things which we talk. Churches of the radical Biblicists have held their heads above the fog of spiritual confusion and remain as those who are able to see clearly.

Martin's book is intended for those who are not well acquainted with Christianity or for those who are confused about which application of Christianity is authentic. It is well adapted to private counseling with individuals who are seeking for truth, or to study in a group of seekers who have little Bible knowledge. This is not intended to be a book for reading pleasure, but as a tool in laying the foundation of Biblical faith. Although Martin's book does not address all details of Christian living, it is intended to help seekers to begin "to observe all things whatsoever I [Christ] have commanded you" (Matt. 28:20). It is designed to clear the fog so the seeker will be able to see clearly and begin to walk rightly.

If you attempt to use this book as a teaching guide for instructing others, you will need to walk the things that you talk. You will be most effective if you sacrifice much time to help the seeker to walk with you. "Be ye doers of the Word and not hearers only" (James 1:22) applies to each one of us individually and to all of us collectively. May God bless this book as a tool in your hands.

- Lester M. Burkholder
Allentown, PA

FOREWORD

Sanctify the Lord God in your hearts: and be ready always to give an answer to every man that asketh you a reason of the hope that is in you with meekness and fear (1 Peter 3:15).

Christians have always been questioned about why we believe what we believe. Why we do some things or refrain from doing other things. It appears to others that our behavior is related to faith-based issues of the heart rather than personal preference. How do we respond?

Having been involved with a men's prison Bible study for more than a decade, there seems no end to the questions asked about the Christian faith and, more specifically, my personal Christian faith. "What do you believe, and why is it different from what other professing Christians practice?" "What right or mandate do you have to believe that you are correct in your practice of Christianity, and by default make other Christians seem less correct in their practice?" These questions, especially when asked in an accusing or derogatory manner, tend to put one on the defensive. They are hard questions. If my way of living Christianity is only based on personal preference and not grounded in the Word of God, then I have no reasonable defense for my practice.

Traditional thought indicates that the further to the right a Christian is theologically, the more literal the approach to Bible doctrine.

As a "Radical Biblicist", I recognize that I am definitely to the right in literal everyday practice of New Testament directives as compared to nominal Christianity. The word "radical" as found in this writing takes the position that the Bible, the Word of God, is inspired by God, it is authentic in its content, its counsel has authority, it was inerrant in the original writings and is our only infallible rule of faith and practice. The definition of a "Biblicist" is a person who seeks to mold their personal life after precepts and principles taught by the Bible in its entirety without attempting to mold those biblical principles and precepts to fit previous denominational and doctrinal teachings. Admittedly, this is a difficult task because over our life spans we have each developed a frame of reference that may or may not have been based on truth.

When confronted with the simple directives of God's Word, principles and applications of Christian living may have to be rethought or discarded.

Why does a radical Biblicist take a different position on issues concerning Christian living that is unlike the position of countless others who profess Christ as their personal Savior?

I identify with Old Testament Joseph when he was asked to interpret the dream of Pharaoh. His answer was,

> It is not in me: God shall give Pharaoh an answer of peace (Genesis 41:16).

Likewise, the answers that I find do not come from within me, but rather from God through the Holy Spirit as I study His Word.

I sincerely hope that, as you read, you find answers of peace, not necessarily easy answers but true answers, for living the victorious Christian life based on the eternal Word of God.

-Arvin Martin

If you are a believer or seeker wanting help to walk the talk, it is available at the following locations.
Phone: (866) 803-6283
http://www.anabaptists.org/clp/locator.html

Chapter 1
THE PURPOSE

Everything exists for a purpose. Buildings exist for housing and shelter, cars exist because of a need for transportation, and businesses exist because of a need for the services that they offer. Printing shops, furniture builders, grocery stores, computer manufacturers all perform services that we need (or at least have learned to rely upon) and are willing to purchase and use.

Occasionally we need a service or product for which we can find no supplier. When such is the case, then we make do without, create it ourselves, or find someone who can provide it for us. There must be a purpose for a service or product to exist. Sometimes a manufacturer puts out a product that seems marketable, but finds in time that there is no market for the product and cannot sell it. Or worse yet, he cannot give it away. The product had no reason to exist.

Man exists. We are here. Therefore man, the only one of God's creation with reasoning power, asks legitimate questions, such as, "Why do I exist? or for what purpose was I born and how do I fulfill that purpose?"

There are a number of questions that are called the "Great Questions of Life." These questions address the very core of our existence. We will examine four of them, using the light of the Word of God for our answers.

1. WHO AM I?

This question can be answered on many levels. We are children of these two parents, from this family, of that community, of a certain ethnic group, or of this country, even to the Latin biological classification, *Homo sapiens*. This does not really tell us who we are. It is simply a classification of where we find ourselves in relation to the plant and animal kingdoms. It tells us nothing of our history, or the purpose for our placement on this planet.

We are created beings with unique qualities. Genesis explains that mankind is a product of the mind of God, created on the sixth day.

How were we created? God tells us how.

> God said, Let us make man in our image, after our likeness: and let them have dominion over the fish of the sea, and over the fowl of the air, and over the cattle, and over all the earth, and over every creeping thing that creepeth upon the earth. So God created man in his own image, in the image of God created he him; male and female created he them (Genesis 1:26-27).

> The LORD God formed man of the dust of the ground, and breathed into his nostrils the breath of life; and man became a living soul (Genesis 2:7).

God created us out of the dust of the earth, and breathed into our nostrils the breath of life, and we became alive - body, soul and spirit. Man, upon creation, was immediately walking, living, breathing, thinking, and communicating. No evolution, just instantly and immediately living in the image of God.

Counter to what some people claim, man did not have to learn to communicate beginning with grunts and gestures before developing a spoken and intelligible language. Adam and Eve were able to communicate with each other and with God the very day they were created.

2. WHY AM I HERE?

(A) FOR GOD'S PLEASURE.

> Thou art worthy, O Lord, to receive glory and honor and power: for thou hast created all things, and for thy pleasure they are and were created (Revelation 4:11).

God, with His creative power, decided to create the solar system, the earth, weather patterns, nature and mankind. Why? Because He could, and because it brought Him pleasure to do so. For this same reason, personal satisfaction, we too might spend years of time and lots of money on a certain project. Creation was a satisfying project to God. It did not take Him decades to complete it, nor did He need someone to finance it.

> By him were all things created, that are in heaven, and that are in earth, visible and invisible, whether they be thrones, or dominions, or principalities, or powers: all things were created by him, and for him: and he is before all things, and by him all things consist (Colossians 1:16-17).

(B) TO BRING GLORY TO GOD.

> Give unto the LORD, O ye mighty, give unto the LORD glory and strength. Give unto the LORD the glory due unto his name; worship the LORD in the beauty of holiness (Psalm 29:1-2).

God is asking us to recognize all His wonderful works and give Him glory for them. Without His creative powers we would not exist. It glorifies God when we are thankful to Him and bless the name of Him in Whom we live, and move, and have our being.

(C) TO WORSHIP GOD.

> Now, Israel, what doth the LORD thy God require of thee, but to fear the LORD thy God, to walk in all his ways, and to love him, and to serve the LORD thy God with all thy heart and with all thy soul, to keep the commandments of the LORD, and his statutes (Deuteronomy 10:12-13).

To walk in awe of Jehovah God, to travel in the paths He has laid out for us and to love Him, and serve Him with all we possess, is worship in the purest form. In true worship there can be no pretense, no half-heartedness, no ignoring or stalling, but rather attentiveness to His commandments and laws.

New Testament passages add to our understanding means to worship God in spirit and in truth. The Holy Spirit w... was given to the New Testament believers greatly added to the worship experience.

(D) TO SERVE OTHERS.

> Bear ye one another's burdens, and so fulfill the law of Christ (Galatians 6:2).Brethren, ye have been called unto liberty; only use not liberty for an occasion to the flesh, but by love serve one another (Galatians 5:13).

We are not on this earth to promote our own agenda, but God's. If God is over all and King of our lives, our ambitions will become subservient to the will and program of God.

We should recognize the fact that God loves others just as much as He loves us. God wants to use us to help them.

(E) TO FOLLOW JESUS CHRIST.

> When he had called the people unto him with his disciples also, he said unto them, Whosoever will come after me, let him deny himself, and take up his cross, and follow me. For whosoever will save his life shall lose it; but whosoever shall lose his life for my sake and the gospel's, the same shall save it (Mark 8:34-35).

Jesus, being the Word of God in human flesh, was the perfect example of how to live. When we need direction on how to respond to circumstances or difficult situations, we will benefit in studying the life of Jesus. The methodology of Jesus cannot be improved upon, for He as the head of the church is the faultless example of Christian living.

Yet for those who have a desire to do God's will, following Christ is not always an easy task. We have a carnal nature. We want to do what we want, how we want, when we want, and not before we want to! It is not painless to give up our wills in preference to someone else. It simply does not sit well with our sinful nature to follow a Christ-like example of non-resistance and love. We would much rather retaliate.

(F) TO PREACH THE GOSPEL.

> Ye shall receive power, after that the Holy Ghost is come upon you: and ye shall be witnesses unto me both in Jerusalem, and in all Judaea, and in Samaria, and unto the uttermost part of the earth (Acts 1:8).

Those who have a personal relationship with God through His son, Jesus, are commanded to tell others about Him. The word gospel means good tidings or good news. If we have found that the Lord is good, we will want to tell others so that they may experience the same joy and peace.

> He [Jesus] said unto them, Go ye into all the world, and preach the gospel to every creature (Mark 16:15).

3. WHERE AM I GOING?

Good question, where are we going? Do we have any way of finding out? Man has always had an endless fascination with life beyond this one. Stories and tales about the hereafter abound;

however, the only sure information we can learn about the hereafter is found in the Word of God. We get glimpses from accounts that are simply written as fact, such as King Saul's encounter with the witch of Endor (1 Samuel 28) and the account Jesus gave about the rich man and Lazarus (Luke 16). We have more words of Jesus and some other enlightening passages in the Book of Revelation. Beyond what has been revealed by the Word is simply speculation and imagination. However, we have been given more than enough to know what to expect, and enough to make sound decisions that will insure a secure, happy existence in eternity. Below are just a few of the many verses that give us insight into the next world.

> It is appointed unto men once to die, but after this the judgment (Hebrews 9:27).

God, the righteous judge, will pass sentence on the way we've lived in relation to the instruction He has given us.

> We must all appear before the judgment seat of Christ; that every one may receive the things done in his body, according to that he hath done, whether it be good or bad (2 Corinthians 5:10).

> Marvel not at this: for the hour is coming, in the which all that are in the graves shall hear his voice, and shall come forth; they that have done good, unto the resurrection of life; and they that have done evil, unto the resurrection of damnation (John 5:28-29).

There are many who heartily wish that when they die, they will die as an animal, being nothing more or less than dead. It is their convenient fantasy that there is no afterlife. If there is no life here after, then we certainly cannot be called into future judgment for our conduct while living on this earth. Countless people have deluded themselves and others into believing this theory. This would be true if human beings were only flesh, but they fail to reckon with the soul which lives forever.

4. IS THERE MORE TO LIFE THAN THIS?

Of course there is. In a physical sense, we may find ourselves in a situation that seems impossible to change or alleviate. For instance, in terminal illness, death creeps closer and closer with no way to stop it. But we can die with a hope of the future.

One of the most well-known scripture verses ever quoted has become well-known for a reason. It is a verse which throws a life preserver to a dying soul. It offers more than we presently have. It offers an opportunity other than eternal death. That verse is John 3:16.

> For God so loved the world, that he gave his only begotten Son, that whosoever believeth in him should not perish, but have everlasting life.

Yes, there is more to life than what we presently have! We have here an offer of everlasting life that just keeps getting better and better. God loves His children and wants the best for them. What could be better than spending eternity with the greatest Father of all?

> Whosoever drinketh of the water that I shall give him shall never thirst; but the water that I shall give him shall be in him a well of water springing up into everlasting life (John 4:14).

> Now being made free from sin, and become servants to God, ye have your fruit unto holiness, and the end everlasting life. For the wages of sin is death; but the gift of God is eternal life through Jesus Christ our Lord (Romans 6:22:23).

We have considered who we are, why we are here, and where we are going. Next, we will consider what took place in early history, which is the basis for why things are the way we presently find them. This is not a theological study of the relationship between God and Satan, or how and why God allows Satan to have the influence that he has in the world. It is only to explain that God does allow Satan to do what he does and how Satan's influence affects us.

Study and Discussion Questions:

1. *In respect to creation, who are we?*
2. *Why are we here?*
3. *What is the destiny of every person?*
4. *Who is the only giver of eternal life?*
5. *What does it mean to have eternal life?*

Chapter 2 FROM THE BEGINNING TO AD 1

We are presently living in the 21st Century since Christ. That equals 2000 years. According to a scripturally derived time line, the earth, a created dwelling for His created creatures, is somewhat over 6,000 years old. There are undoubtedly some who will read this book and be horrified to find that there are those who still do not subscribe to the theory of evolution.

Virtually all of the theories in vogue in the early 1900s are now obsolete. Man can theorize, build models, and wear out computers in their effort to understand what happened at creation. But for every finding that seemingly points to evolution, another finding validates the Word of God.

The Christian rests on the Word of the Lord of the Universe Who was there at creation, and Who elected to tell some things about it. To believe that everything we see somehow sprang into being without an intelligent designer stretches the imagination beyond limits. There must be a cause, a force, an intelligent design, for such a complex universe to be brought into existence. Cars do not just happen, nor do airplanes. Several generations have witnessed the process of computers being developed over the past decades. Documented history proves that they did not just happen to exist. Neither did flowers, birds, nor people which are infinitely more complex.

Discoveries in astronomy and physics have shown beyond reasonable doubt that our universe did in fact have a beginning. Theologians and scientists alike assert that before Genesis 1:1, nothing that we can measure in our natural realm existed: there was no space, time, matter, or energy. The beginning was a supernatural event based outside of the realm of human comprehension. The question that begs for an answer is not whether there is a universe, but rather how and when did it begin? The book of Hebrews states that things are not as they seem on the surface.

> Through faith we understand that the worlds were framed by the word of God, so that things which are seen were not made of things which do appear (Hebrews 11:3).

If one could have walked up to Adam on the seventh day of creation, when he was one day old, human reasoning would have concluded that in appearance he was about 25 years old. Such reasoning would be wrong because he was not as old as the usual criteria of human aging would lead one to believe. The same applies to the world, mountains, seas, and galaxies.

The radical Biblicist is more than willing to accept God's explanation. Therefore the basis of this book rests on foundation principles as recorded in Genesis.

In the beginning God created a perfect world. The first chapter of Genesis states six times that what God created was good. Finally, in the last verse God pronounced it very good. It could not be improved upon. God was the author of this perfection. There could be no credit given to man for the perfect peace and rest that all creation then experienced.

Life was simple. There was no sweat, no searching for food, no eight or ten hour shifts at work, no wardrobe to maintain, no one to impress, no drought, no thunderstorms, no tornados, no houses to fall apart, no heating bills, no taxes, no becoming old, and no death.

Sometime following those first days, a created being, an angel, called a serpent, but more commonly known as Satan, or Lucifer, became jealous of God and His power and made plans to usurp his Creator's authority and power.

> How art thou fallen from heaven, O Lucifer, son of the morning! how art thou cut down to the ground, which didst weaken the nations! For thou hast said in thine heart, I will ascend into heaven, I will exalt my throne above the stars of God: I will sit also upon the mount of the congregation, in the sides of the north: I will ascend above the heights of the clouds; I will be like the most High. Yet thou shalt be brought down to hell, to the sides of the pit (Isaiah 14:12-15).

God defeated his plans and has fixed his destiny. Meanwhile God has allowed earth to be his domain for a definite period of time, after which he will spend eternity in everlasting torment.

> Then shall he say also unto them on the left hand, Depart from me, ye cursed, into everlasting fire, prepared for the devil and his angels (Matthew 25:41).

Satan continues to hate God and righteousness, and spends full time trying to get man to worship and give allegiance to himself. God, our Creator, is the rightful owner of our praise, adoration and obedience.

God's creation: earth, and especially man, from the first days of history became the battleground between the forces of God and the forces of evil. The battle is for control of the souls of men.

Satan cannot physically harm or get to God personally in any way. Satan is a created being with limited power. His power lies only in the area of theft. We are God's property:

> Know ye that the LORD he is God: it is he that hath made us, and not we ourselves; we are his people, and the sheep of his pasture (Psalm 100:3).

We are His sheep with the freedom of choice. God has given His sheep everything they need to be happy and content.

Satan, through lies and deceit, paints a picture of a life that is far superior to the one that God has provided for us. He is a "sheep thief," and he has been quite successful at it. Remember, the end of the life that Satan offers is eternal death.

In a successful effort to get man to turn away from God the creator, the serpent came to Eve and suggested that God was something less than good. He suggested that God was withholding wonderful knowledge from them. He falsely promised that they would become better people, and become as gods by eating the fruit of the tree of the knowledge of good and evil. Also, true to form, he told them straight out that God was lying when He said that they would surely die.

> The serpent was more cunning than any beast of the field which the LORD God had made. And he said to the woman, "Has God indeed said, 'You shall not eat of every tree of the garden'?" And the woman said to the serpent, "We may eat the fruit of the trees of the garden; but of the fruit of the tree which is in the midst of the garden, God has said, 'You shall not eat it, nor shall you touch it, lest you die.'" Then the serpent said to the woman, "You will not surely die. For God knows that in the day you eat of it your eyes will be opened, and you will be like God, knowing good and evil."
>
> So when the woman saw that the tree was good for food, that it was pleasant to the eyes, and a tree desirable to make one wise, she took of its fruit and ate. She also gave to her husband with her, and he ate. Then the eyes of both of them were opened, and they knew that they were naked; and they sewed fig leaves together and made themselves coverings (Genesis 3:1-7 NKJV).

The moment Adam and Eve ate the fruit in disobedience to God's direct command, their future on earth immediately changed. They instantly started to age and deteriorate physically. Death came into their experience. The woman would have pain in childbirth, and was to be ruled by man.

> To the woman He said: "I will greatly multiply your sorrow and your conception; in pain you shall bring forth children; your desire shall be for your husband, and he shall rule over you" (Genesis 3:16 NKJV).

For the man, the earth was cursed. It would no longer grow plants the way it did before. Noxious weeds appeared to thwart man's farming efficiency. The strength of the whole world seemed to have lost its potency.

> To Adam He said, "Because you have heeded the voice of your wife, and have eaten from the tree of which I commanded you, saying, 'You shall not eat of it': cursed is the ground for your sake; in toil you shall eat of it all the days of your life. Both thorns and thistles it shall bring forth for you, and you shall eat the herb of the field. In the sweat of your face you shall eat bread till you return to the ground, for out of it you were taken; for dust you are, and to dust you shall return" (Genesis 3:17-19 NKJV).

Man also became estranged from God spiritually; the perfect relationship was hopelessly broken. Man had no means to restore the relationship. He was driven from the Garden of Eden never to return. As a man might break a priceless, one of a kind, irreplaceable crystal bowl, so Adam and Eve broke the relationship with God through rebellion and disobedience.

> Therefore the LORD God sent him out of the Garden of Eden to till the ground from which he was taken. So He drove out the man; and He placed cherubim at the east of the Garden of Eden, and a flaming sword which turned every way, to guard the way to the tree of life (Genesis 3:23-24 NKJV).

God became distant and Satan capitalized on this broken relationship by luring humanity to a life of rebellion against God. In our fallen natures, we are more inclined to listen to Satan than to God. However, God has always faithfully called to His children, reminding them of the blessings of obedience and warning those who are impenitent in their rebellion and disobedience.

> Like as I pleaded with your fathers in the wilderness of the land of Egypt, so will I plead with you, saith the Lord GOD (Ezekiel 20:36).

During this time frame, God was establishing His moral code. What does the word "moral" mean? It means, "of or relating to principles of right and wrong in behavior."

Is there right or wrong behavior? If so, by whose standard; that of the community, the government, the local judge, the minister, or the church? Who has the right to judge human conduct? The answer: Almighty God, Who established the code.

If one is of the persuasion that evolution is true and humans are just a complex level of random accidents, then why and how did the moral code make its appearance? Why are there those who believe in the sanctity of life? Why are there state and federal laws forbidding murder? If we are just some half-cooked, constantly evolving primordial slime, then there is really no basis for concern about murder, theft, rape, suicide, euthanasia, or abortions.

God has not left us with such an option. God presupposes in His conversation with Adam that he is capable of disobedience. As soon as Satan made his appearance and presented the possibility of making the wrong decision (taking and eating the fruit), the issue became a moral one.

God is true and if He says "follow this path," and Satan a liar says "no, follow this path," then we have a decision to make. There are only two paths, and we must choose which path to take. If the one way honors our Creator and the other way is disobedient to our Creator, then the one way is right and the other is wrong. Therefore the decision becomes a moral issue of right and wrong.

Suppose you sit down for breakfast and you wish to eat cold cereal. In front of you are two boxes of lawfully purchased cereal. All other things being equal, there are no moral implications of you choosing one brand over the other. You decide and choose the one you like best.

If, however, you know that the one box was stolen, there is a moral implication. If you should decide to eat the stolen cereal rather than the lawfully purchased one, you have made a moral decision. Deciding not to return the stolen one to the rightful owner is condoning theft. At that point it becomes a moral issue, for the scripture states plainly, "Thou shalt not steal." Remember, moral issues are defined by right and wrong as determined by God.

God gave the moral code from the very beginning. These are called foundational principles or creation principles. They were given for all mankind everywhere. They are not just Judeo-Christian principles; they are God's principles.

To name a few:

1. ORDER IS GOOD, CHAOS IS NOT.

God said His work was very good.

> And God saw every thing that he had made, and, behold, it was very good. And the evening and the morning were the sixth day (Genesis 1:31).

2. ORGANIZATION OF THE HOME; HEADSHIP ORDER (God, father, mother, children).

Unto the woman he said, I will greatly multiply thy sorrow and thy conception; in sorrow thou shalt bring forth children; and thy desire shall be to thy husband, and he shall rule over thee. And unto Adam he said, Because thou hast hearkened unto the voice of thy wife, and hast eaten of the tree, of which I commanded thee, saying, Thou shalt not eat of it: cursed is the ground for thy sake; in sorrow shalt thou eat of it all the days of thy life (Genesis 3:16, 17).

3. PROPERTY RIGHTS.

And God blessed them, and God said unto them, Be fruitful, and multiply, and replenish the earth, and subdue it: and have dominion over the fish of the sea, and over the fowl of the air, and over every living thing that moveth upon the earth (Genesis 1:28).

4. ESTABLISHMENT OF GOVERNMENT.

And surely your blood of your lives will I require; at the hand of every beast will I require it, and at the hand of man; at the hand of every man's brother will I require the life of man. Whoso sheddeth man's blood, by man shall his blood be shed: for in the image of God made he man (Genesis 9:5, 6).

5. INSTITUTION OF MARRIAGE

Therefore shall a man leave his father and his mother, and shall cleave unto his wife: and they shall be one flesh (Genesis 2:24).

6. WEARING OF CLOTHING

And the eyes of them both were opened, and they knew that they were naked; and they sewed fig leaves together, and made themselves aprons. And they heard the voice of the LORD God walking in the garden in the cool of the day: and Adam and his wife hid themselves from the presence of the LORD God amongst the trees of the garden. And the LORD God called unto Adam, and said unto him, Where art thou? And he said, I heard thy voice in the garden, and I was afraid, because I was naked; and I hid myself. And he said, Who told thee that thou wast naked? Hast thou eaten of the tree, whereof I commanded thee that thou shouldest not eat? Unto Adam also and to his wife did the LORD God make coats of skins, and clothed them (Genesis 3:7-11, 21).

7. SANCTITY OF LIFE.

And the LORD said unto Cain, Where is Abel thy brother? And he said, I know not: am I my brother's keeper? And he said, What hast thou done? the voice of thy brother's blood crieth unto me from the ground. And now art thou cursed from the earth, which hath opened her mouth to receive thy brother's blood from thy hand; when thou tillest the ground, it shall not henceforth yield unto thee her strength; a fugitive and a vagabond shalt thou be in the earth (Genesis 4:9-12).

8. DAY OF REST

> And on the seventh day God ended his work which he had made; and he rested on the seventh day from all his work which he had made. And God blessed the seventh day, and sanctified it: because that in it he had rested from all his work which God created and made (Genesis 2:2, 3).

These principles are held by virtually all nations and peoples everywhere, and they were practiced by nations of antiquity.

On Mount Sinai God gave Moses the law that included moral standards and rules to live by, including the Ten Commandments. These laws are still the basis for the moral code today. They established a God-given benchmark by which to measure human behavior.

God deeply desired that His creation, fallen humanity, return to Him. He went to great lengths to give the Children of Israel rules and guiding principles to live by. How else would they know what pleased their Creator if there were no tenets to give direction to establish right from wrong?

At the end of creation week, the relationship God had with man was absolutely perfect. By God's own description it was very good. The fact that it was very good indicates that no sin, no rebellion, no broken relationships were yet a part of their experience. Man was walking with God with a beautiful, unmarred relationship.

How well we know that this is no longer the case. Is it possible to regain the perfect, healthy relationship that was lost so many years ago?

In this beautiful relationship with God, He gave only one restriction.

> The LORD God took the man, and put him into the garden of Eden to dress it and to keep it. And the LORD God commanded the man, saying, Of every tree of the garden thou mayest freely eat: but of the tree of the knowledge of good and evil, thou shalt not eat of it: for in the day that thou eatest thereof thou shalt surely die (Genesis 2:15-17).

In Genesis 3 Satan came to Eve and enticed her through lies to rebel against God and to break the only restriction they had. She succumbed to his enticement and ate of the fruit. She gave to Adam and he ate also. Immediately there was a long fall from where they were to where man is presently.

Man is now out of fellowship with God, earning his bread by the sweat of his face, working to pay for all the things he needs. He experiences drought, thunderstorms, houses that fall apart, bills without end, taxes galore, sickness and death with no peace or rest. It was a long, hard fall, and it exists in vivid color still today. There is debauchery, lust, and evil on every hand.

Man is quite incapable, on his own, of changing or undoing the damage that he has done. He is lost, disobedient, living in sin, with no ability to change the "mess" he has made.

It is as though we have fallen from the main floor of a house, (a perfect relationship with God) down the steps into the basement (broken relationship with God). We are now lying on the floor of the basement wounded, bruised, broken, unable to move, looking up the steps to where we used to be. God has not moved; we are the ones who have fallen through disobedience. We do not have the ability or the strength to climb the stairs back into a right relationship with God. If we do not get help, we will die on that basement floor. We have not just fallen, we have fallen hard.

This is the situation in which Adam and Eve found themselves. No hope, no strength and no self improvement plan.

But wait, God had a plan. We are familiar with the term "God's plan of redemption" or perhaps "God's provision of salvation." God has executed a plan for our rescue, healing, and deliverance from sin. It is a plan that reached down the steps and gave us hope of being delivered from certain death. God began to introduce the plan immediately after the fall. It was more than just a plan, it was a provision. It was nothing mankind did or deserved, but God still loved us even though we had failed miserably. His love was so great that immediately after the fall of Adam and Eve He pointed to a day when this relationship would be restored.

> I will put enmity between thee and the woman, and between thy seed and her seed; it shall bruise thy head, and thou shalt bruise his heel (Genesis 3:15).

The first step toward reconciliation was the introduction of the blood sacrifice. God instituted the blood sacrifice for the remission of sins, giving man a way to have an acceptable relationship with Him. If man in faith and obedience offered burnt offerings, God was pleased with such conduct. Starting with Abel, men of God offered burnt offerings to God: Noah, Abraham, Isaac, and Jacob. God told Moses:

> The life of the flesh is in the blood: and I have given it to you upon the altar to make an atonement for your souls: for it is the blood that maketh an atonement for the soul (Leviticus 17:11).

Many years later, Jesus Christ, the perfect Lamb of God, would fulfill, through His shed blood and death, the requirement of the Old Testament blood sacrifice.

> But God commendeth his love toward us, in that, while we were yet sinners, Christ died for us (Romans 5:8).

Abraham, a man of God, because of his strong faith and obedience was promised that through his lineage the whole earth would be blessed. This was fulfilled in the coming of Jesus Christ.

> In thy seed shall all the nations of the earth be blessed; because thou hast obeyed my voice (Genesis 22:18).

Moses pointed ahead to Jesus when he said:

> The LORD thy God will raise up unto thee a Prophet from the midst of thee, of thy brethren, like unto me; unto him ye shall hearken (Deuteronomy 18:15).

One step at a time, God was promising and delivering a way to a restored relationship with Him. Job longed for the day when there would be a mediator to improve the relationship between God and man.

> Nor is there any mediator between us, who may lay his hand on us both (Job 9:33 NKJV).

God gave laws and rules to the nation of Israel, which if followed in faith, would collectively and individually direct the people in a way that was pleasing to Him.

While obedience brought God's blessing upon His people, they were still far removed from the original relationship with Him.

Even though the Spirit of God did not rest on all the people, there were those of the Old Testament era who followed closely after Him. God Himself testifies to the excellent relationship He enjoyed with some of the men of long ago.

Enoch walked with God.

> Enoch walked with God: and he was not; for God took him (Genesis 5:24).

Abraham was called the friend of God.

> The scripture was fulfilled which saith, Abraham believed God, and it was imputed unto him for righteousness: and he was called the Friend of God (James 2:23).

Moses was a man with whom God talked face to face.

> There arose not a prophet since in Israel like unto Moses, whom the LORD knew face to face (Deuteronomy 34:10).

King David was a man after God's own heart.

> He raised up unto them David to be their king; to whom also he gave testimony, and said, I have found David the son of Jesse, a man after mine own heart, which shall fulfill all my will (Acts 13:22).

Job was perfect and upright before God.

> There was a man in the land of Uz, whose name was Job; and that man was perfect and upright, and one that feared God, and eschewed evil (Job 1:1).

Daniel was beloved of God.

> At the beginning of your supplications the command went out, and I have come to tell you, for you are greatly beloved; therefore consider the matter, and understand the vision (Daniel 9:23 NKJV).

Even these God-fearing men had only begun to move toward the unbroken relationship Adam and Eve experienced before their fall in the garden.

Note a few Old Testament passages where God spoke through prophets to promise a remedy for improved relationships between Him and man.

> The voice of him that crieth in the wilderness, Prepare ye the way of the LORD, make straight in the desert a highway for our God. Every valley shall be exalted, and every mountain and hill shall be made low: and the crooked shall be made straight, and the rough places plain: And the glory of the LORD shall

> be revealed, and all flesh shall see it together: for the mouth of the LORD hath spoken it (Isaiah 40:3-5).

God Himself has spoken it; it will come to pass.

> For unto us a child is born, unto us a son is given: and the government shall be upon his shoulder: and his name shall be called Wonderful, Counselor, The mighty God, The everlasting Father, The Prince of Peace. Of the increase of his government and peace there shall be no end, upon the throne of David, and upon his kingdom, to order it, and to establish it with judgment and with justice from henceforth even for ever. The zeal of the LORD of hosts will perform this (Isaiah 9:6-7).

How we long for peace! O Lord, hasten the day when the relationship that was broken is fully restored!

> In the days of these kings shall the God of heaven set up a kingdom, which shall never be destroyed: and the kingdom shall not be left to other people, but it shall break in pieces and consume all these kingdoms, and it shall stand for ever (Daniel 2:44).

Many more Old Testament verses pointed to the time when God would again take further measures to improve our relationship with Him. Prophecy regularly indicated a great day that was still to come. The last two verses of the Old Testament read like this:

> Behold, I will send you Elijah the prophet before the coming of the great and dreadful day of the

> LORD: and he shall turn the heart of the fathers to the children, and the heart of the children to their fathers, lest I come and smite the earth with a curse (Malachi 4:5-6).

Then all was quiet for 400+ years. Had God forgotten His promises?

Study and Discussion Questions:

1. *What separated man and woman from a meaningful relationship with God?*
2. *Whose property are we?*
3. *What has God provided for the happiness of mankind?*
4. *What were the curses God placed upon Satan, Eve, and Adam?*
5. *How did each one's punishment fit their individual sin?*
6. *Who is the remedy for fallen, sinful man?*

Chapter 3
FROM AD 1 TO THE END

> And he shall bring forth a son, and thou shalt call his name JESUS: for he shall save his people from their sins. Now all this was done, that it might be fulfilled which was spoken of the Lord by the prophet, saying, Behold, a virgin shall be with child, and shall bring forth a son, and they shall call his name Emmanuel, which being interpreted is, God with us (Matthew 1:21-23).

Starting with this announcement, the next 35 years would bring long awaited provisions for the restoration of the relationship between God and man. God's plan was designed to be fulfilled within His own time-frame.

Simeon, while blessing the Christ child in the temple, declared these words:

> Lord, now lettest thou thy servant depart in peace, according to thy word: for mine eyes have seen thy salvation, which thou hast prepared before the face of all people; a light to lighten the Gentiles, and the glory of thy people Israel (Luke 2:29-32).

John the Baptist spoke these words while preaching by the river Jordan:

> I indeed baptize you with water unto repentance: but he that cometh after me is mightier than I, whose shoes I am not worthy to bear: he shall baptize you with the Holy Ghost, and with fire: whose fan is in his hand, and he will throughly purge his floor, and gather his wheat into the garner; but he will burn up the chaff with unquenchable fire (Matthew 3:11-12).

Jesus' birth, life, death, resurrection, and ascension, have been steps to restore man's relationship with God.

Jesus' birth confirmed that there was a plan in place for man's salvation. This was verified by God, angels, and men who wrote of the event. It was also a confirmation of the words of the prophets, written more than 400 years before.

Jesus' whole life was a sermon calling men to return to God.

> Jesus answered and said unto him, If a man love me, he will keep my words: and my Father will love him, and we will come unto him, and make our abode with him (John14:23).

He also spoke about the true state of the heart.

> A good man out of the good treasure of the heart bringeth forth good things: and an evil man out of the evil treasure bringeth forth evil things (Matthew 12:35).

> To love him [God] with all the heart, and with all the understanding, and with all the soul, and with all the strength, and to love his neighbor as himself, is more than all whole burnt offerings and sacrifices (Mark 12:33).

Because it was the sacrifice of the perfect, sinless Lamb of God, Jesus' death was the last blood sacrifice that was needed. Sins were no longer merely covered, they were taken away.

> John seeth Jesus coming unto him, and saith, Behold the Lamb of God, which taketh away the sin of the world (John 1:29)

Jesus' resurrection broke the stranglehold of eternal death. He has given us the power and possibility to live an endless life.

> For God so loved the world, that he gave his only begotten Son, that whosoever believeth in him should not perish, but have everlasting life (John 3:16).

Each event of Christ's life brings us closer to the possibility of the original relationship that was lost through Adam's sin. But we must believe in Him and follow Him.

Jesus offered His assistance to those who had a desire to have a right relationship with God.

> Come unto me, all ye that labor and are heavy laden, and I will give you rest. Take my yoke upon you, and learn of me; for I am meek and lowly in heart: and ye shall find rest unto your souls. For my yoke is easy, and my burden is light (Matthew 11:28-30).

After Jesus ascended back to heaven, He sent the promised Holy Spirit Who now dwells in each believer. The promise, spoken by Ezekiel the prophet and later by Jesus, was fulfilled.

> I will give them one heart, and I will put a new spirit within you; and I will take the stony heart out of their flesh, and will give them an heart of flesh: that they may walk in my statutes, and keep mine ordinances, and do them: and they shall be my people, and I will be their God (Ezekiel 11:19-20).

True believers are living in fulfillment of this prophecy. Peace is restored in the heart of the Christian, but we still have our sinful natures to crucify every day, and there is still depravity on every hand. We are not home yet. There is more to come. We are still looking for a land wherein dwells righteousness without sin, where all things are made new.

Abraham, in faith, looked ahead to a time when he would dwell with God in the city of God.

> By faith he sojourned in the land of promise, as in a strange country, dwelling in tabernacles with Isaac

> and Jacob, the heirs with him of the same promise: For he looked for a city which hath foundations, whose builder and maker is God (Hebrews 11:9-10).

We, too, look for a better place than anything we have experienced to date.

> For here have we no continuing city, but we seek one to come (Hebrews 13:14).

John the Revelator saw a vision of the city for which Abraham longed, and for which we also continue to look.

> I saw a new heaven and a new earth: for the first heaven and the first earth were passed away; and there was no more sea. And I John saw the holy city, new Jerusalem, coming down from God out of heaven, prepared as a bride adorned for her husband. And I heard a great voice out of heaven saying, Behold, the tabernacle of God is with men, and he will dwell with them, and they shall be his people, and God himself shall be with them, and be their God. And God shall wipe away all tears from their eyes; and there shall be no more death, neither sorrow, nor crying, neither shall there be any more pain: for the former things are passed away. And he that sat upon the throne said, Behold, I make all things new (Revelation 21:1-5).

What does God require of Christians to be assured of this wonderful promise of a totally restored relationship?

On what basis will we be judged? What determines where we will spend eternity? Do we need only to believe that Jesus is the

Son of God? After a man accepts Jesus as his personal Savior, what comes next? Is there a life to be lived?

God does give us direction. The chapters ahead will address some basic principles the New Testament has given for instruction in living the Christian life.

Study and Discussion Questions:

1. *Upon what condition may one be baptized?*
2. *How does the heart affect human conduct?*
3. *How did the resurrection break the stranglehold of eternal death?*
4. *Explain how Jesus' yoke is easy.*
5. *How do we acquire "one heart" and "a new spirit"?*

Chapter 4
THE BASIS

> [The church is] built upon the foundation of the apostles and prophets, Jesus Christ himself being the chief corner stone (Ephesians 2:20).

Every building, if it is to endure long, needs a good, solid foundation. Jesus, spoke about two houses, one having been built upon a rock and the other built on sand. One withstood the storm but the other did not.

> Therefore whosoever heareth these sayings of mine, and doeth them, I will liken him unto a wise man, which built his house upon a rock: and the rain descended, and the floods came, and the winds blew, and beat upon that house; and it fell not: for it was founded upon a rock. And every one that heareth these sayings of mine, and doeth them not, shall be likened unto a foolish man, which built his house

> upon the sand: and the rain descended, and the floods came, and the winds blew, and beat upon that house; and it fell: and great was the fall of it. (Matthew 7:24-27).

Most builders desire to build something substantial, something that will stand the test of time. A large stone or steel structure may last a few hundred years. The longer an architect wishes a building to stand, the more sure the foundation must be and the more durable the building material. A concrete foundation will last longer than a wooden foundation. A stone wall will last longer than one of plywood, and brick lasts longer than drywall. Some cheaply built houses are worthless in twenty years, but a stone cathedral may last five hundred years or more. But even they will eventually crumble into the dust. The pyramids of Egypt, the Parthenon of Greece, the Stonehenge of England, all were glorious structures in their time, but now many are in disrepair or ruins.

What will last? What is forever? In what can we place our confidence that will endure? We are eternal souls. But what provisions, what abode, what existence will be provided for us a million years from now?

Who and what are forever?

God is forever.

> Before the mountains were brought forth, or ever thou hadst formed the earth and the world, even from everlasting to everlasting, thou art God (Psalm 90:2).

The Word of God is forever.

> For ever, O LORD, thy word is settled in heaven (Psalm 119:89).

> The word of the Lord endureth for ever. And this is the word which by the gospel is preached unto you (1 Peter 1:25).

The kingdom of God and His son Jesus is forever.

> There was given him dominion, and glory, and a kingdom, that all people, nations, and languages, should serve him: his dominion is an everlasting dominion, which shall not pass away, and his kingdom that which shall not be destroyed (Daniel 7:14).

The mercy of the Lord upon them that fear Him is forever.

> The mercy of the LORD is from everlasting to everlasting upon them that fear him, and his righteousness unto children's children (Psalm 103:17).

Heaven is forever. God has provided a place of rest for the never-dying soul of every man.

The saints shall reign with Jesus in Heaven forever. Those who love and serve Him will find everlasting bliss and peace in heaven. They will spend eternity in heaven in a perfect relationship with God and Jesus Christ.

> I heard a great voice out of heaven saying, Behold, the tabernacle of God is with men, and he will dwell with them, and they shall be his people, and God himself shall be with them, and be their God. And God shall wipe away all tears from their eyes; and there shall be no more death, neither sorrow, nor crying, neither shall there be any more pain: for the former things are passed away (Revelation 21:3-4).

> There shall be no night there; and they need no candle, neither light of the sun; for the Lord God giveth them light: and they shall reign for ever and ever (Revelation 22:5).

Hell is forever.

Everlasting punishment is awaiting the disobedient and those who have rejected God's rightful claim on their lives.

> As the Father hath life in himself; so hath he given to the Son to have life in himself; and hath given him authority to execute judgment also, because he is the Son of man. Marvel not at this: for the hour is coming, in the which all that are in the graves shall hear his voice, and shall come forth; they that have done good, unto the resurrection of life; and they that have done evil, unto the resurrection of damnation (John 5:26-29).

> If any man worship the beast and his image, and receive his mark in his forehead, or in his hand, the same shall drink of the wine of the wrath of God, which is poured out without mixture into the cup of his indignation; and he shall be tormented with fire and brimstone in the presence of the holy angels, and in the presence of the Lamb: and the smoke of their torment ascendeth up for ever and ever: and they have no rest day nor night, who worship the beast and his image, and whosoever receiveth the mark of his name (Revelation 14:9-11).

We have a choice between heaven and everlasting punishment. There is no third option. We cannot stay on earth, because it will be destroyed. There will not be a world as we know it. This world had a beginning and God says it will have an end.

> The heavens and the earth, which are now, by the same word, are kept in store, reserved unto fire against the day of judgment and perdition of ungodly men (2Peter 3:7).

Everything that we do, if it is to have blessing of God, must be built on the right foundation. If we wish to spend eternity with Jesus, we must live a life that is pleasing to God. What pleases God? Can we know? Yes, we can know!

Study and Discussion Questions:

1. *What on earth is eternal?*
2. *Who is eternal?*
3. *What is eternal?*
4. *What are the only two destinies of man?*
5. *Who has a rightful claim to our lives?*

Chapter 5
TO BE IS TO DO

Suppose you had met and spent a day with a man who told you he was a law enforcement officer. As you questioned him, you learned that he was not employed by any agency, and did not have a firearm or badge. He did not behave himself in a professional manner, nor did he seem to respect the law. He did not appear to have even a basic knowledge of law enforcement protocol. What would you think as you parted? Was he really an officer or not? His claims did not meet the expectations of what you knew about law enforcement. Would you hesitate to take his claims at face value? You might conclude he was only fooling himself or delusional, and rightly so.

Now carry this concept into the area of Christianity. Is it wise for us to willingly take people at face value when the walk does not even closely resemble the talk? Is it because we believe in being generous, or are we not sure in ourselves what constitutes Christianity? Are we called to a walk of faith only, or is it necessary to have visible evidences to support our claim?

Once a person is saved (born into the family of God), the next logical question is: How do I stay saved and have the assurance of eternity in heaven with Jesus Christ? What must I do to stay saved, or is it a once and done deal? Are there rules to live by?

There are different avenues of thought concerning this subject. Some people say salvation is by faith alone; others say that salvation is by works, while others say that it doesn't matter either way. This can be quite confusing. What does the Word of God say?

It has been said, "For every mile of road, there are two miles of ditches." On this subject there is a mile of "faith ditch" on one side of the road and a mile of "works ditch" on the other. Satan is not concerned about which ditch we fall into; to him one ditch is as good as the other. If a flawed understanding pulls us into the "faith only" ditch or into the "works only" ditch, it is all the same to him. Satan is pleased that we are no longer making progress on the Christian pathway, but we are stuck in a ditch.

It is quite easy to raise one aspect of Christian living to a higher place than is warranted, and diminish other aspects that are just as important. Satan wants us to become unbalanced, and then continue on that course until our relationship with God becomes compromised and finally becomes void. He wants us to get a fixation on one aspect at the expense of the others.

Three thoughts seem to be prevalent in modern Christendom.

1. NEITHER FAITH NOR WORKS IS IMPORTANT.

When God is finished with us here, we are all going to heaven anyway. (When a person dies, no matter what he has believed or how he has lived, someone will say, "Well, he is certainly in a better place.") This is very convenient and embraced by many people, because it is comforting to believe that all will be well in the afterlife. Unfortunately, this is heresy of the highest order, and absolutely unsupported by Scripture.

2. FAITH IS IMPORTANT.

Scriptures used to support this position are:

> By grace are ye saved through faith; and that not of yourselves: it is the gift of God: not of works, lest any man should boast (Ephesians 2:8-9).
>
> Believe on the Lord Jesus Christ, and thou shalt be saved, and thy house (Acts 16:31).

Many men and women profess Christianity and give a glowing testimony of how the Lord has worked in their lives, yet show little difference from the world in either conduct or dress.

"Just have faith and believe," they say, "and that is all that is required." They want no cross, no sense of responsibility to live a holy life, and no restraints for the sake of Jesus and the Gospel. This perception of Christian living is alive and well in liberal Christianity.

3. WORKS AND MORE WORKS ARE IMPORTANT.

Supporters of this position draw from verses such as:

> What doth it profit, my brethren, though a man say he hath faith, and have not works? can faith save him (James 2:14)?

> [Paul] showed first unto them of Damascus, and at Jerusalem, and throughout all the coasts of Judaea, and then to the Gentiles, that they should repent and turn to God, and do works meet for repentance (Acts 26:20).

Jesus once gave the Pharisees a stiff reprimand.

> Woe unto you, scribes and Pharisees, hypocrites! for ye pay tithe of mint and anise and cummin, [works] and have omitted the weightier matters of the law, judgment, mercy, and faith: these ought ye to have done, and not to leave the other undone (Matthew 23:23).

The Pharisees lived in the works ditch (since they had not believed on Jesus to begin with). The same still goes on today.

Some Christians forget they were saved by faith in Jesus Christ and turn to trusting church membership or trusting the keeping of certain rules for their salvation. They know very little of a life that has been resurrected with Christ, a Holy Spirit filled life, a joyful life, and victorious Christian living.

What is the proper position on the faith and works issue? Acts 10-11 introduces a man named Cornelius.

> There was a certain man in Caesarea called Cornelius, a centurion of the band called the Italian band, a devout man, and one that feared God with all his house, which gave much alms to the people, and prayed to God always. He saw in a vision evidently about the ninth hour of the day an angel of God coming in to him, and saying unto him, Cornelius. And when he looked on him, he was afraid, and said, What is it, Lord? And he said unto him, Thy prayers and thine alms are come up for a memorial before God. And now send men to Joppa, and call for one Simon, whose surname is Peter: he lodgeth with one Simon a tanner, whose house is by the sea side: he shall tell thee what thou oughtest to do (Acts 10:1-6).

Cornelius was a seeking man who feared God, had a devotional life, prayed, gave alms, and fasted. Many good Christians fail to meet this level of religious fervor.

Cornelius had a God-awareness that produced works, but he needed to put his faith in Jesus. If the knowledge he had was enough, God would not have told him to contact Peter.

> Who [Peter] shall tell thee words, whereby thou and all thy house shall be saved (Acts 11:14).

If this account had taken place ten years earlier, before Jesus had died on the cross for our sins, what Cornelius was doing would likely have been sufficient. But with the coming of Jesus those works were no longer sufficient. Cornelius did not know salvation meant having faith in the shed blood of Jesus Christ that could take away his sins. God was faithful to see that he received the information he needed to have a right relationship with God.

> Neither is there salvation in any other: for there is none other name (Jesus) under heaven given among men, whereby we must be saved (Acts 4:12).

> Knowing that a man is not justified by the works of the law, but by the faith of Jesus Christ, even we have believed in Jesus Christ, that we might be justified by the faith of Christ, and not by the works of the law: for by the works of the law shall no flesh be justified (Galatians 2:16).

Works without faith will not render us innocent, or free, or just, or righteous in the sight of God. Works do not equal salvation. What part then, does works play?

> And again He entered Capernaum after some days, and it was heard that He was in the house. Immediately many gathered together, so that there was no longer room to receive them, not even near the door. And He preached the word to them.

> Then they came to Him, bringing a paralytic who was carried by four men. And when they could not come near Him because of the crowd, they uncovered the roof where He was. So when they had broken through, they let down the bed on which the paralytic

> was lying. When Jesus saw their faith, He said to the paralytic, "Son, your sins are forgiven you" (Mark 2:1-5 NKJV).

The scripture says "when Jesus saw their faith." Faith! How do we know they had faith? We see it in their works. Works is faith in shoe leather!

The four men carrying the man with paralysis knew that if they could get him to Jesus he would be healed. Faith! Because of this, when they couldn't get him through the crowd, they did not sit down and have a conference, saying, Look this man is a pretty serious case. It is likely Jesus cannot heal such a serious disease anyway. It's too much bother taking off the roof; let's just say it was a bad plan, go home, and call it a day.

Works are a confirmation of our faith! If we have faith, the fruit, works, will follow.

> What doth it profit, my brethren, though a man say he hath faith, and have not works? can faith save him? If a brother or sister be naked, and destitute of daily food, And one of you say unto them, Depart in peace, be ye warmed and filled; notwithstanding ye give them not those things which are needful to the body; what doth it profit? Even so faith, if it hath not works, is dead, being alone. Yea, a man may say, Thou hast faith, and I have works: shew me thy faith without thy works, and I will shew thee my faith by my works. Thou believest that there is one God; thou doest well: the devils also believe, and tremble. But wilt thou know, O vain man, that faith without works

> is dead? Was not Abraham our father justified by works, when he had offered Isaac his son upon the altar? Seest thou how faith wrought with his works, and by works was faith made perfect? And the scripture was fulfilled which saith, Abraham believed God, and it was imputed unto him for righteousness: and he was called the Friend of God. Ye see then how that by works a man is justified, and not by faith only. Likewise also was not Rahab the harlot justified by works, when she had received the messengers, and had sent them out another way? For as the body without the spirit is dead, so faith without works is dead also (James 2:14-26).

We are saved by faith, but we will be judged by our works. The tree of Faith bears fruit and this fruit is called Works.

> We must all appear before the judgment seat of Christ; that every one may receive the things done in his body, according to that he hath done, whether it be good or bad (2 Corinthians 5:10).

> Other foundation can no man lay than that is laid, which is Jesus Christ. Now if any man build upon this foundation gold, silver, precious stones, wood, hay, stubble; every man's work shall be made manifest: for the day shall declare it, because it shall be revealed by fire; and the fire shall try every man's work of what sort it is. If any man's work abide which he hath built thereupon, he shall receive a reward. If any man's work

> shall be burned, he shall suffer loss: but he himself shall be saved; yet so as by fire (1 Corinthians 3:11-15).

Our works are to be a testimony to others, proving our faith.

> Having your conversation honest among the Gentiles: that, whereas they speak against you as evildoers, they may by your good works, which they shall behold, glorify God in the day of visitation (1 Peter 2:12).

Works prove what we have deep down in our hearts.

> Doth a fountain send forth at the same place sweet water and bitter? Can the fig tree, my brethren, bear olive berries? either a vine, figs? so can no fountain both yield salt water and fresh. Who is a wise man and endued with knowledge among you? let him shew out of a good conversation [life] his works with meekness of wisdom (James 3:11-13).

Paul had only one question for the Galatians:

> This only would I learn of you, Received ye the Spirit by the works of the law, or by the hearing of faith (Galatians 3:2)?

The correct Scriptural position is: We are saved by faith in Jesus Christ. As a result, we receive the outpouring of the Holy Spirit which produces good works through us. We read the Scripture and do what it says. This is proving our faith by our works.

Yea, a man may say, Thou hast faith, and I have works: show me thy faith without thy works, and I will show thee my faith by my works (James 2:18).

Study and Discussion Questions:

1. *Is it wise for us to assume that people are Christians when their walk does not even closely resemble their talk? Is it wise for us to assume they are not?*
2. *How do I acquire assurance of salvation?*
3. *How do I retain assurance of salvation?*
4. *Is faith important? How about works?*
5. *What is the relationship between faith and works?*
6. *On what basis will we be judged?*

Chapter 6
THE WORD OF GOD

The sincere Christian has a very high regard for the written Word of God, the Bible. We believe it is the message from God. If we want to know God and to know His thoughts, that information is found within the pages of the Holy Bible. We also believe that the Word of the Lord will endure forever.

> For ever, O LORD, thy word is settled in heaven (Psalm 119:98).

We also do not believe that the Bible only contains the word of God, but rather that the Bible IS the Word of God.

There are those who treat the Bible like a food bar in a restaurant. I'll have a big helping of this sugar-coated love, which is so good. No, I really don't care much for discipline, it just upsets my stomach. Did you try the health and wealth smothered with whipped cream? It's the best! Do not try the "come out and be separate." I tried it once and it made me half dizzy.

When there is a "pick and choose" attitude toward the Word, all Scripture becomes subjective. We decide what is worthwhile and what is not. When it does not line up with our theology or make us feel great, we discard it.

Paul writing to Timothy said:

> All scripture is given by inspiration of God, and is profitable for doctrine, for reproof, for correction, for instruction in righteousness: that the man of God may be perfect, throughly furnished unto all good works (2 Timothy 3:16-17).

Since all Scripture is inspired by God, should New Testament Christians hold that both Testaments are equal in regard to our belief and practice?

In the Sermon on the Mount, Christ declared that He is the fulfillment of the Old Testament, and the Old Testament patriarchs looked forward to the time of Christ. Therefore, we believe the teachings of the New Testament supersede the teachings of the Old Testament.

We must maintain a very high regard for the Old Testament in that it teaches us many things and points us to Christ. We also recognize that there is Old Testament prophecy that is to this day unfulfilled. There are many lessons we can learn from Old Testament accounts. We learn not only of God's faithfulness and longsuffering toward all mankind, but also of His sure punishment for sin and rebellion.

> Whatsoever things were written aforetime were written for our learning, that we through patience and comfort of the scriptures might have hope (Romans 15:4).

Are New Testament people bound to the Ten Commandments of the Old Testament? The truth is that Jesus has raised the bar to a much higher standard in the New Testament which supersedes the Old. There are over 1,000 commandments in the New Testament. Five times in the Matthew 5, Jesus taught, "It hath been said . . . but I say unto you . . ." The Old Testament called attention to the people's hearts of stone. The prophets foretold a day when those hearts of stone would be removed and replaced with hearts of flesh, ones that would be sensitive to the prompting of the Holy Spirit.

> You, being dead in your sins and the uncircumcision of your flesh, hath he quickened together with him, having forgiven you all trespasses; blotting out the handwriting of ordinances that was against us, which was contrary to us, and took it out of the way, nailing it to his cross; and having spoiled principalities and powers, he made a show of them openly, triumphing over them in it (Colossians 2:13-15).

> It was symbolic for the present time in which both gifts and sacrifices are offered which cannot make him who performed the service perfect in regard to the conscience concerned only with foods and drinks, various washings, and fleshly ordinances imposed until the time of reformation (Hebrews 9:9, 10 NKJV).

The Old Testament law was in effect until the time of the death of Jesus Christ, the Lamb of God who offered the perfect blood sacrifice. Now animal sacrifices and ceremonial washings are no longer necessary.

New Testament Christians concern themselves with New Testament writings in order to discern how to live in the New Testament era. We are free from the Old Testament laws and rituals. Old Testament saints were not "Christians" per se because there was no Jesus to emulate. We, as New Testament Christians, have at our fingertips the teachings of Jesus and the inspired confirmations and practical applications of these truths by the New Testament writers. We are not free from the responsibilities that are a necessary part of the Christian life.

It is imperative that New Testament Christians take seriously the teachings of the New Testament writers. Since all Scripture is given by inspiration of God, we cannot afford to ignore portions of Scripture simply because they do not seem to fit well with the brand of Christianity we desire.

If the Scripture gives us direction concerning a certain area of Christian living, then there must be a way to put it into everyday practice. Jesus did not give us commands that are impossible to keep. Sometimes practices differ between Christian groups but with God's Word as the standard and the Holy Spirit to guide us, there must be a way to make these truths practical.

So often, when discussing a practical command of the New Testament, someone will say, "But that was for back then." Or, "It was a cultural thing. We are way past that now." Nowhere is it found that Jesus or the apostles put a time limit on teachings such as: Christian modesty and non-resistance shall be null and void after the year AD 1900.

No time limits are found on the restrictions or commands of the New Testament, with the exception of when Jesus returns again and old things pass away. In light of this fact, all of us could use help in honestly living the life of a believer and follower of Jesus Christ as the New Testament writers defined it for us.

> Blessed are they that do his commandments, that they may have right to the tree of life, and may enter in through the gates into the city (Revelation 22:14).

Of which set of commandments is John speaking? Would it not be fair to believe that they are the ones that Jesus gave us while on earth, as well as the ones He gave to us through the Apostles? How many of the commandments in the inspired Word of God, which God has so graciously given to us for spiritual direction, can we ignore or explain away before we lose our right to the tree of life and be turned away at the gate of the city?

Study and Discussion Questions:

1. *How do we know the Bible is God's inspired Word?*
2. *What do we learn from the Bible?*
3. *Why is the New Testament on a higher level than the Old Testament today?*

Chapter 7
THE HOLY SPIRIT

The Lord never intended that New Testament Christians should live their lives without the indwelling of the Holy Spirit. From Old Testament times the prophets spoke of a day when the people of God would be filled with the Spirit.

> A new heart also will I give you, and a new spirit will I put within you: and I will take away the stony heart out of your flesh, and I will give you an heart of flesh. And I will put my spirit within you, and cause you to walk in my statutes, and ye shall keep my judgments, and do them (Ezekiel 36:26-27).

While Jesus was on the earth, He spoke of the time He would leave the world and send the Holy Spirit to indwell His people. In the book of John, He calls the Holy Spirit the Comforter.

> The Comforter, which is the Holy Ghost, whom the Father will send in my name, he shall teach you

> all things, and bring all things to your remembrance, whatsoever I have said unto you (John 14:26).

One of the last things Jesus told them before He was taken up to heaven was to wait in Jerusalem until the Holy Spirit came upon them. They were not to leave town until they were filled with the Holy Spirit.

> Being assembled together with them, he [Jesus] commanded them that they should not depart from Jerusalem, but wait for the promise of the Father, which, saith he, ye have heard of me. For John truly baptized with water; but ye shall be baptized with the Holy Ghost not many days hence (Acts 1:4-5).

This should be a warning to us. We cannot live a successful victorious Christian life without the Holy Spirit. We do not have enough willpower, enough wisdom, enough grace, enough strength or enough love to live a life that is acceptable to God.

It is the Spirit Who guides us into truth.

> When he, the Spirit of truth, is come, he will guide you into all truth: for he shall not speak of himself; but whatsoever he shall hear, that shall he speak: and he will show you things to come (John 16:13).

It is the Spirit Who gives us words to say that honor God in hard situations.

> When they deliver you up, take no thought how or what ye shall speak: for it shall be given you in that same hour what ye shall speak. For it is not ye that

> speak, but the Spirit of your Father which speaketh in you (Matthew 10:19-20).

It is the Holy Spirit Who gives us direction in the work of the Lord.

> The Spirit said unto Philip, Go near, and join thyself to this chariot (Acts 8:29).
>
> While Peter thought on the vision, the Spirit said unto him, Behold, three men seek thee (Acts 10:19).

It is the indwelling of the Holy Spirit that causes us to possess and exhibit the fruit of the Spirit.

> The fruit of the Spirit is love, joy, peace, longsuffering, gentleness, goodness, faith, meekness, temperance: against such there is no law. And they that are Christ's have crucified the flesh with the affections and lusts (Galatians 5:22-24).

It runs contrary to our fleshly desires to forgive those who abuse us; we want revenge. It is against human nature to return good for evil; but if we follow the path of Jesus, this is what we are called to do.

> I say unto you which hear, Love your enemies, do good to them which hate you, Bless them that curse you, and pray for them which despitefully use you. And unto him that smiteth thee on the one cheek offer also the other; and him that taketh away thy cloke forbid not to take thy coat also. Give to every man that asketh of thee; and of him that taketh away thy

> goods ask them not again. And as ye would that men should do to you, do ye also to them likewise (Luke 6:27-31).

Attempting to live the Christian life without being filled with the Holy Spirit is an exercise in futility. It is the Holy Spirit that gives us the "want to." It is the Holy Spirit that gives us wisdom, boldness, and direction.

> Be not drunk with wine, wherein is excess; but be filled with the Spirit (Ephesians 5:18).

The Holy Spirit guides in understanding the Word of God; He never takes away from it or directs contrary to the Word of God. Occasionally people claim that the Spirit told them, contrary to the teaching of the New Testament. God the Father, God the Son, and God the Holy Spirit are One. There is no confusion, no double talk, no ambiguity, no smoke and mirrors. They are in perfect harmony!

> There are three that bear record in heaven, the Father, the Word, and the Holy Ghost: and these three are one (1 John 5:7).

THE CONSCIENCE

No discussion about the Holy Spirit would be complete without addressing the topic of the conscience. What role does a person's conscience have in the life of a Christian? The Holy Spirit uses the conscience to guide the believer into right paths of action. What is the conscience?

Someone has said,

> A conscience is a knowledge or sense of right and wrong, with a compulsion to do right; moral judgment that opposes the violation of a previously recognized ethical principle and that leads to feelings of guilt if one violates such a principle.

Conscious is a God-awareness that was instilled into us by the breath of God, giving us abilities the rest of creation does not have.

> The LORD God formed man of the dust of the ground, and breathed into his nostrils the breath of life; and man became a living soul (Genesis 2:7).

With this divine breath operating in us, we have a God-awareness of right and wrong. The Holy Spirit uses the conscience to work in the area between what we know to be the standard of right and truth, and where we actually are relative to what we have just done. He uses the conscience to prompt our thoughts and actions and judge our plans. If it is the wrong action or motive, He convicts us. He can use it to help us determine right from wrong and steer us into a way that pleases God. A true follower of God will desire a sensitive conscience, one that is open to the leading of the Holy Spirit. The radical Christian strives to have a clear conscience, one free from guilt. However, as God is always working with us to bring us closer to Him, our conscience is always active and prompting us about wrong thoughts, wrong words, wrong attitudes, or lack of personal devotions, etc. We should never wish our conscience would quit working, for God uses it to keep us in check against evil.

We live along a railroad track that is about 90 yards from the house. We have a big tire rim near the track, next to our garden, in which we burn garden trash, vines, leaves, etc. If the weather is dry, I drag a garden hose from the house to have nearby to keep the fire under control. Because of resistance with 300 feet of hose, I have very little pressure at the nozzle. Hardly enough with which to fight a fire, but it makes me feel good to have it there. When I open the valve, I get a small stream of water at low pressure. It would barely be enough to make me wet, but I have water.

Carrying this concept into the realm of the gift of the Holy Spirit, should it be necessary for me to assure others that I indeed am filled with the Spirit? Is it because it is such a small trickle, and there are so many restrictions and kinks in the hose that they cannot be sure unless I tell them? If I am filled with the Spirit, I will be exhibiting such fruit of the Spirit that they will know.

I have been privileged to know many godly, Spirit-filled men and women, but it would be well-nigh impossible to get them to flaunt the fact. One of the fruits of the Spirit is meekness. Godly people never boast that the Spirit is moving in their lives. These men and women realize the relationship with God through the Spirit is sacred. It is so humbling that God would be pleased to dwell in mortal man that they could never brag about it. It is about God, not man. The Holy Spirit has no entertainment value, nor is He a personal servant Whom we can make to work for us at will. As the Spirit moves in a church service, we are not to be proud, but humbled, that the Lord chooses to manifest Himself to His unworthy servants.

> Thus saith the high and lofty One that inhabiteth eternity, whose name is Holy; I dwell in the high and holy place, with him also that is of a contrite and humble spirit, to revive the spirit of the humble, and to revive the heart of the contrite ones (Isaiah 57:15).

That the Spirit of God would be pleased to dwell in a man is a sacred thing. He is worthy of our humble and grateful praise.

Study and Discussion Questions:

1. *What name did Jesus give the Holy Spirit?*
2. *What were the purposes of sending the Holy Spirit?*
3. *What are the values of our conscience?*
4. *What is the fruit of the Holy Spirit?*

Chapter 8
HOW SHALL WE THEN LIVE?

On the next page is a diagram. On the right side is God's position which I am designating the Zero position. Under the Zero position is a subject and under the subject are some Bible verses that give God's thoughts on the subject. These positions that God has identified in the Bible cannot be improved upon. This is the standard of holiness and practical living that the New Testament Christian is called to accept as their standard of living. On any subject, we cannot say that God has gone too far in His expectations or that He did not go far enough, or that somehow we can improve on what was written. Anything we do that differs from God's standard would move us away from God's desire for our behavior.

The closer we walk to the stated position of God the closer we are to the center of His perfect will for our lives. The less we obey His standard, the farther we get from His will on the matter.

BLACK GRAY WHITE

THE LINE

-10 Evil	-5 Gray Area	0 Safe/Sane Position
	Grace/Freeboard ⟷	
Disobedience / Sin		Obedience / Righteousness
Of the World		Separation II Cor. 6:17, 18; I John 3:3
Pride / Jewelry / Undress		Humility / Modesty I Pet. 3:3; I Tim. 2:9, 10
Retaliation		Nonresistance I Thess. 5:15; I Pet. 3:9
Idols / Pornography / Sexually Explicit Websites, Books or Films, etc.		No Wicked Thing Before My Eyes Ps. 101:3; Ps. 125:5
Uncovered Head / Cut Hair		The Christian Woman's Headship Veiling I Cor. 11:5, 6
Divorce / Remarriage / Homosexuality / Fornication		One Man and One Woman for Life Mark 10:6-12; Romans 1:26-27

Underneath the Zero position you find the words Obedience / Righteousness. Underneath the -10 position on the chart you will see the words, Disobedience / Sin. In between these positions you will find a -5, and underneath it a title called gray area. Somewhere in this gray area there is a line that separates the saved from the lost. As a person moves away from obedience to God's stated position into an area that is in disobedience to God's stated position, eventually in their moving they cross this line. At some point, their disobedience becomes such that they are no longer a child of God but rather a rebellious child of Satan. There is an old poem that explains this truth quite well.

THE HIDDEN LINE (The Destiny of Men)

**There is a time, we know not when,
A point we know not where,
That marks the destiny of men
To glory or despair.
There is a line by us unseen,
That crosses every path;
The hidden boundary between
God's patience and his wrath.
To pass that limit is to die–
To die as if by stealth;
It does not quench the beaming eye
Or pale the glow of health.
The conscience may be still at ease,
The spirit lithe and gay;
That which pleases still may please,
And care be thrust away.
But on that forehead God has set,
Indelibly a mark
Unseen by men, for men as yet
Are blind and in the dark.**

And yet the doomed man's path below
May bloom as Eden bloomed;
He did not, does not, will not know,
Or feel that he is doomed.
He knows, he feels that all is well,
And every fear is calmed;
He lives, he dies, he wakes in hell,
Not only doomed, but damned.
Oh, where is this mysterious bourn
By which our path is crossed;
Beyond which God himself hath sworn,
That he who goes is lost.
How far may we go on in sin?
How long will God forbear?
Where does hope end, and where begin
The confines of despair?
An answer from the skies is sent,
"Ye that from God depart,
While it is called today, repent,
And harden not your heart."
Joseph Addison Alexander (1809-1860)

On the right side you will find a horizontal line that starts at the Zero position and goes to the "line." This is captioned "Grace/ Freeboard." The word "grace" in this application means being in God's favor as a Christian while trying to do what is right, even though we are less than perfect. We can never attain, as humans, to the perfect standard of excellence that God has given to us. But as long as we have an honest heart and are sensitive to the direction of the Holy Spirit, God accepts us as righteous. We are all in a learning experience, and we all have room to grow.

> But grow in grace, and in the knowledge of our Lord and Savior Jesus Christ (2 Peter 3:18).

Grace is given to the honest heart to cover the discrepancies between intent and actuality. We are accepted as righteous in God's sight.

However, presuming on the grace of God in willful sin is extremely dangerous. To sin and depend somehow on the grace of God to nullify the sin, fails to take into consideration the law of sowing and reaping. We reap the consequences of a sinful life. Paul asks the question in Romans 6:1-2:

> What shall we say then? Shall we continue in sin, that grace may abound? God forbid. How shall we, that are dead to sin, live any longer therein?

On the diagram the word "freeboard" is next to the word grace. Freeboard is a nautical term defining the distance between the waterline and the main deck of a ship, or between the level of the water and the upper edge of the side of a small boat. If there are three people in a small boat designed for two, the extra person would overload the boat and cause it to sit lower in the water. With a dangerously small amount of freeboard, the boat could easily be swamped. Any quick move or large wave could sink the boat.

Carry this concept into the spiritual life. The closer a person is to the perfect will of God, and the less amount of baggage they have in the boat with them, the higher the boat sits in the water and the more freeboard there is. Therefore they are in a safer position. Grace (freeboard) covers the sudden waves of Satan and the un-premeditated sin. The further a person gets from obedience to the commandments, and the higher their tolerance for sin (baggage), the more they have in the boat with them. Consequently their boat sits lower in the water (less freeboard) and the easier it is for Satan to swamp their boat. At some point, grace, like freeboard, will no longer keep them from destruction. They have allowed the baggage (sin) to accumulate to the point of no remedy (no deliverance).

> They mocked the messengers of God, and despised his words, and misused his prophets, until the wrath of the LORD arose against his people, till there was no remedy (2 Chronicles 36:16).

This was God speaking in the Old Testament to His chosen people. He was saying that they finally crossed the line; the day of grace for them was over. They chose to disregard God and His precepts until He directed His anger towards them.

> He that despised Moses' law died without mercy under two or three witnesses: of how much sorer punishment, suppose ye, shall he be thought worthy, who hath trodden under foot the Son of God, and hath counted the blood of the covenant, wherewith he was sanctified, an unholy thing, and hath done despite unto the Spirit of grace (Hebrews 10:28, 29)?

This passage is speaking of Christians (they were once sanctified) who have continued in sin after conversion. They have wandered far away from the will of God. They have become more laden with sin (no freeboard remains) until they capsize and drown in their sin.

If the Old Testament people were stoned for despising Moses' law, what horrible punishment will await those carnal "Christians" who despise the blood of Jesus, their Savior?

Our only recourse is, with a transformed heart, to know and be obedient to God's directives in the New Testament, and to obey the leading of the Holy Spirit. In this way, we are accepted of God.

Study and Discussion Questions:

1. *How can the believer know God's will in a matter?*
2. *After one is born again, is it right to continue practicing sinning? Why?*
3. *If we continue sinning knowingly, what are the dangers?*
4. *What are the consequences for continuing to sin?*
5. *Is there forgiveness for the practice of sin?*

Chapter 9 PRACTICAL HOLINESS

On the chart are listed six areas of practical Christian living. We will explore each Biblical teaching and then discuss how to apply it. These are some of the areas where radical Christians come out differently in their practice than most modern day Christians.

-10	-5	0
Of the World	|	Separation
		2 Corinthians 6:17, 18; 1 John 3:3

To God who knows and understands all things including the thoughts and intents of the heart, there is no gray area; it is either black or white. Either it is sin, or it is not sin. It is not hard for God to establish a Zero position. We, who were born with sinful natures and evil tendencies, do not find it so easy. We must go to God's Word for direction.

What does the Word of God have to say about how a Christian (a person who has dedicated his life to the service of Jesus) is to relate to the evil society that surrounds him? Every Christian must understand that most of the people they meet do not share many of the same values they do. The Christian's highest calling is to live for God, but the compelling force of the men and women of the world is to please self.

For the believer, God's Word is clear:

> Come out from among them, and be ye separate, saith the Lord, and touch not the unclean thing; and I will receive you, and will be a Father unto you, and ye shall be my sons and daughters, saith the Lord Almighty (2 Corinthians 6:17-18).

> Have no fellowship with the unfruitful works of darkness, but rather reprove them (Ephesians 5:11).

We, as Christians, have a mandate to separate ourselves from the evil thinking and deeds of society. We cannot become involved in the filthy, sinful practices of the world and be a son or daughter of God. We cannot become involved with programs or practices of the world that sap our strength and zeal for things of spiritual value. Sports, politics, entertainment, and the arts, have little, if any, eternal value and they can do much damage to the kingdom of God.

Make no mistake, these things are interesting and entertaining. It is easy to become enthralled by people's skills, intelligence or abilities to perform. However, we cannot let these things control our affections, for then they become idols. Some Christians are so taken up with sports, money, or antiques that they can talk of nothing else. These obsessions siphon off time and energy making it more difficult for Christians to be excited about eternal things.

On Judgment Day, will God be impressed if I spent a million dollars on a rare painting? Does missing a worship service for the purpose of spending Sunday on my boat, tractor, at the ballpark, or at the parade give any indication as to the possibility of having my values out of line?

Christians are not only to be different in degree (moderate use of good things), but in action. There are some things we may not do. We are now serving Christ instead of self.

> Lie not one to another, seeing that ye have put off the old man with his deeds; and have put on the new man, which is renewed in knowledge after the image of him that created him (Colossians 3:9-10).

> If any man be in Christ, he is a new creature: old things are passed away; behold, all things are become new (2 Corinthians 5:17).

> Whatsoever ye do in word or deed, do all in the name of the Lord Jesus, giving thanks to God and the Father by him (Colossians 3:17).

The old behavior model used when we served self will not fit. The new model is a whole new frame of reference, which is serving Christ and pleasing Him in every area of life. In doing this, the radical Christian is willing to limit himself in the areas of things that are not wrong in themselves, but are not the best things. It may not have been "wrong" for the Prophet Jonah to go on a cruise, but his timing was way off, because God had said, "Go to Nineveh." Taking a cruise to Tarshish at this point was outright disobedience!

> Every man that hath this hope in him purifieth himself, even as he is pure (1 John 3:3)

To be pure and clean we must wash in pure water. As we cannot become clean by washing in a mud puddle, neither can we become clean or stay clean while handling and dealing in the dirty things of this world. Spiritually, there is no purity in the world system. It is controlled by Satan, the father of lies, deception, idolatry and all sorts of filth and debauchery. To find anything pure we have to go to the source of purity. God is the only dealer of pure and clean.

> Let us draw near with a true heart in full assurance of faith, having our hearts sprinkled from an evil conscience, and our bodies washed with pure water (Hebrews 10:22).

Realistically, every Christian becomes spiritually tainted during a day's activity. We are constantly bombarded with impure sights, evil thoughts, notions of pride, covetousness and lust. We are in a battle for our souls, and Satan will spare no effort to take captives.

For this reason the radical Christian is never quite satisfied with his current relationship with God or with his own performance. He realizes that there is always room for more purity and Christ-likeness. Paul, in Philippians 3:13, 14, uses these words:

> Brethren, I count not myself to have apprehended: but this one thing I do, forgetting those things which are behind, and reaching forth unto those things which are before, I press toward the mark for the prize of the high calling of God in Christ Jesus.

We are to leave the old behind and reach out for the new. People who have made the change from the old to the new want no parts of the old. Our flesh still pulls on us wanting to be satisfied, but the spirit that is washed by pure "water," does not want to be spotted by the filth of the world.

> Others save with fear, pulling them out of the fire; hating even the garment spotted by the flesh (Jude 1:23).

Since God hates spotted garments, we ought to hate spotted garments on ourselves, and on our fellow Christians.

Lord, give us the strength to stand in an evil day.

Study and Discussion Questions

1. *What does it mean to be holy?*
2. *How important is holiness to God?*
3. *What is the relationship between separation from the world and holiness?*
4. *To whom should we draw near?*

Chapter 10
HUMILITY

Modesty comes from a heart of humility. Humility expresses itself in modesty. Therefore, it is necessary to examine humility before going further into the subject of modesty. "Humility" and "meekness" are attributes that we enjoy in others but perhaps find difficult or distasteful in ourselves.

These words may suggest images of timidity, indecisiveness, and insecurity. They conjure up mental pictures of someone easily taken advantage of or easily swayed by popular demands. Nothing could be further from the truth! Humility and meekness are not traits of weakness, but come from voluntary and deliberate action. Humility and meekness are vital to a successful and vibrant Christian life.

> Thus saith the high and lofty One that inhabiteth eternity, whose name is Holy; I dwell in the high and holy place, with him also that is of a contrite and

> humble spirit, to revive the spirit of the humble, and to revive the heart of the contrite ones (Isaiah 57:15).

The opposite of humility is pride. Ninety-one Bible verses use the words proud or pride. Never is pride considered a good attribute. God can easily use a humble and contrite person in kingdom work, but not a proud, arrogant one.

> He gives more grace. Therefore He says: "God resists the proud, but gives grace to the humble (James 4:6 NKJV).

Pride blocks the avenue of blessing from God that we so desperately need. Pride is a sin that every Christian must guard against on a regular basis.

It was pride that caused Satan to fall from favor with God. He was the first created being that rebelled against God.

> Thou hast said in thine heart, I will ascend into heaven, I will exalt my throne above the stars of God: I will sit also upon the mount of the congregation, in the sides of the north (Isaiah 14:13).

It was pride and rebellion against the authority of God that caused Adam and Eve to take and eat of the fruit when God had said they should not.

Pride is a foundational sin and can be traced to virtually all other sins. We could diagnose almost every known sin and find a root of pride.

Anger? When I am not getting my way, or feel that I am not being respected, or someone is trying to make me look bad, my pride is being bruised.

> Only by pride cometh contention: but with the well advised is wisdom (Proverbs 13:10).

Adultery? My desires and wants are more important than the desires and wants of my spouse. By breaking my vows made to God and to my spouse, I am lying and causing the other to break their vows. I am relying on the mistaken notion that I deserve anything I can get. This is driven by pride.

Theft? Gratifying my flesh and covetous nature is more important than the rights of the owner.

Slander? I attempt to make someone else seem less desirable, so that I seem smarter or wiser than they.

> Pride goeth before destruction, and an haughty spirit before a fall (Proverbs 16:18).

> A man's pride shall bring him low: but honor shall uphold the humble in spirit (Proverbs 29:23).

The radical Christian realizes that he is nothing without God. Because he has no blessing or advantage that God has not given him, he has nothing to boast about. His strength comes from God; his ability to think and make a living comes from God; his food comes from God; his salvation and his promise of a home in heaven come from God. You name the blessing, it comes from God. There is nothing to be proud of.

The only thing we have to call our own is our sin and rebellious nature. Knowing this, we walk softly and humbly before God. Of ourselves, we have nothing to boast. Pride is not becoming to the life of a Christian. The radical Christian, even though he must daily crucify the sin of pride, lives a life that points to and glorifies God rather than himself.

Our will and what we want is subservient to God's will for our lives. As we will discuss in following chapters, this concept is applied into every area of our Christian life.

> He hath shewed thee, O man, what is good; and what doth the LORD require of thee, but to do justly, and to love mercy, and to walk humbly with thy God (Micah 6:8)?

Study and Discussion Questions:

1. *What is humility?*
2. *What is pride?*
3. *How is expression given to either pride or humility?*
4. *How should we approach God?*
5. *How should we relate with our fellowman?*

Chapter 11
THE UNASSUMING LIFE

-10	-5	0
Pride / Jewelry / Undress	|	Humility / Modesty
		1 Peter 3:3; 1 Timothy 2:9–10

Clothes became needful in the world because of sin. Prior to sin there was no need for clothing. The first couple did not have clothes. There was no evil, no lustful thinking, no coveting, and no immorality of any type anywhere on the earth . . .

> They were both naked, the man and his wife, and were not ashamed (Genesis 2:25).

. . . until they ate the forbidden fruit. Adam and Eve's conscience then spoke to them that they needed to be covered. With sin came knowledge of good and evil. They hid themselves from God and attempted to cover their nakedness.

> When the woman saw that the tree was good for food, and that it was pleasant to the eyes, and a tree to be desired to make one wise, she took of the fruit thereof, and did eat, and gave also unto her husband with her; and he did eat. And the eyes of them both were opened, and they knew that they were naked; and they sewed fig leaves together, and made themselves aprons (Genesis 3:6-7).

The subject of clothes is one with which we are very familiar. Most of us have closets full of them. We dress ourselves before we meet the gaze of society. Each morning we look in our closets and decide what to wear. If we are going to work, we wear these clothes over here; if we are going to church, then we wear those back there. Most of us consciously decide what we are going to wear to any given occasion.

Why does my wardrobe look like it does? How do I decide that one piece of clothing is okay, but another one is not?

Someone has said, "You are what you wear." What I wear is a projection of my self-image.

When we put on clothes, we simultaneously reveal our self-image. We choose how we look unless we are so poor that we have to wear whatever is available. There are clothes that we will not wear because they are "not me". We can deliberately put on clothing that screams, "Look at me!" or clothes that say, "There is nothing for you here; move on."

Some people will wear clothing that sends mixed messages, and they are not aware of it. However, when a person claims to follow Christ but their clothing proclaims immodesty, fashion, or money, which is being more truthful, the walk or the talk, the clothes or what they are saying? Generally speaking, clothes do not lie; they are more accurate to the real state of the spiritual life of the person than verbal proclamations.

Suppose that the next time I fly commercially, I notice that the person slipping into the captain's seat has on a muscle shirt, a skull and crossbones tattoo, captain's hat on backwards, a nose stud and flip-flops? At the very least, I would question the integrity of the company that hired him, and at most I might fear for the safety of the flight and refuse to board.

Clothes tell a story about values. Sometimes clothing says, "This is what I am." At other times it says, "This is what I wish I were." There are clothes that say, "I am a biker, farmer, airline pilot, cowboy, nurse, construction worker, stewardess, prostitute, king, or a fast-food employee." Are there no clothes that say, "I am a child of God"? Actually, there are.

If God is first in our lives, we will want to wear clothes that give an essence of godliness, not an essence of world-mindedness. We are to wear clothing that properly reveals His inner presence, not that which reveals the body.

History shows that women are much more fascinated and captivated by clothes than men. Men have their own fascinations but, normally, clothes do not rate high on their list of priorities.

Notice the standard for Christian women set forth by God in the following verses. Both of these passages are expressly speaking to how wives/women should dress and behave themselves. These are not just suggestions; God fully expects that His children will practice these verses every day.

> Do not let your adornment be merely outward--arranging the hair, wearing gold, or putting on fine apparel, rather let it be the hidden person of the heart, with the incorruptible beauty of a gentle and quiet spirit, which is very precious in the sight of God (1 Peter 3:3-4 NKJV).

God inspired the writers of the New Testament to address the issue of appearance. God knows that the clothing we put on, the way we arrange or cut our hair, and the wearing of jewelry is an indication of what we think of ourselves.

Why do men and women wear jewelry? Jewelry is primarily a status symbol. Again, we come back to the pride factor. Pride as displayed by jewelry says, "I have disposable wealth, I can afford this, I am a person of accomplishment" or "I fit in here" or perhaps "I am superior to you, I am important."

No child of God needs jewelry to prove that they are somebody. A person will be accepted and approved in the eyes of God by unflinching obedience to the guiding principles set forth in His Word. The same goes for tattoos. Our body is the temple of God; we are not free to use our skin as a billboard.

Is the wedding ring an exception which is acceptable because it is a symbol of marriage which was instituted by God? Should it be worn by Christians because it is a token of a vow of fidelity and unfailing love?

There is no Scripture to indicate that a band on the third finger of the left hand is to be used to indicate marital status. Does God want us to be sensitive to His Word, obeying scripture, or does He want us to follow some ritual and symbol that is the product of man's imagination, directly disobeying Bible directives concerning jewelry and pride?

A Christian man or woman who strives to portray the faithfulness of Christ in their life will hardly need a wedding band to keep the opposite sex at bay. Our clothing and demeanor speak louder than a ring on the finger ever will.

There is another verse found in 1st Timothy that uses nearly the same words but in the reverse order.

> In like manner also, that the women adorn themselves in modest apparel, with propriety and moderation, not with braided hair [fancy combings] or gold or pearls or costly clothing, but, which is proper for women professing godliness, with good works (1 Timothy 2:9-10 NKJV).

This verse says that Christians should decorate or beautify themselves with modest apparel. There seems to be no place for tight jeans, low cut blouses, bare midriffs, high heels, jewelry, tattoos, or designer clothes. This verse, if taken at face value, (for women only?) is very straightforward. Do not wear anything that says, "Look at my body."

The Christian who takes God's word seriously, with reserve toward the opposite sex and reverence toward God, will attempt to wear modest, unpretentious clothing. He or she will show self-control and sobriety, without special hair styles, jewelry, or expensive clothing that draws attention.

The Christian church has the responsibility to ask their members to adhere to a dress standard that promotes modesty. We need each other to help keep us unspotted from the world. We are incapable of being aware of all the ways that Satan comes to us with temptations of pride. In order to help us maintain modesty, we need advice from other godly members.

However, as good as a dress standard may be, it cannot of itself win the heart. We may conform to the letter of the law, but totally miss the spiritual principle of modesty. If we have a heart that is bent on displaying the body as a sex object, we can still find many ways to wear the prescribed clothes immodestly, drawing attention to the physical rather than the spiritual.

Jesus weighed in on the issue that the life reflects the heart.

> Ye shall know them by their fruits. Do men gather grapes of thorns, or figs of thistles? Even so every good tree bringeth forth good fruit; but a corrupt tree bringeth forth evil fruit. A good tree cannot bring forth evil fruit, neither can a corrupt tree bring forth good fruit. Every tree that bringeth not forth good fruit is hewn down, and cast into the fire. Wherefore by their fruits ye shall know them (Matthew 7:16-20).

Admit or deny it, what we wear tells a story. While room must be given for growth in the Christian life, the fact remains that our clothes give indication of our respect for Scripture and portray our feelings about ourselves. With our mouth we might say "I am a Christian," but if our apparel does not reflect what we say, we present a confusing message regarding our professed identity with Jesus.

Study and Discussion Questions:

1. *Why did Adam and Eve wear no clothes?*
2. *Why were they not ashamed?*
3. *Why did they become ashamed and hide?*
4. *What do clothes and makeup tell others about you?*
5. *Does God care about what we wear?*

Chapter 12 NONRESISTANCE

-10	-5	0
Retaliation	|	Nonresistance *I Thess. 5:15; I Pet. 3:9*

One of the clearest and most disregarded of Jesus' teachings is the command not to seek revenge when we have been wronged.

This teaching and concept is so strongly at odds with our carnal fighting tendency and our vengeful nature that it is simply too difficult for the natural man to comprehend. To state it simply, turning the other cheek is just not the way we are inclined to settle our differences.

Although the New Testament teaches much about nonresistance, we like to see examples. No example is more striking than that of Jesus as He endured suffering in His trial and on the cross. How could Jesus, Who had thousands of angels standing by, available at a prayer's breath, allow a few of His sinful creatures to abuse Him and nail Him to the cross to die?

> Then said Jesus unto him, Put up again thy sword into his place: for all they that take the sword shall perish with the sword. Thinkest thou that I cannot now pray to my Father, and he shall presently give me more than twelve legions of angels (Matthew 26:52-53)?

Not only did He willingly submit to this, but He gave His followers command to put the sword away. Before His crucifixion, He had more to say to His followers in the Sermon on the Mount.

> I say unto you, That ye resist not evil: but whosoever shall smite thee on thy right cheek, turn to him the other also (Matthew 5:39).

The following verse is given to us by Apostle Paul.

> See that none render evil for evil unto any man; but ever follow that which is good, both among yourselves, and to all men (1 Thessalonians 5:15).

Apostle Peter also wrote on the issue,

> Not rendering evil for evil, or railing for railing: but contrariwise blessing; knowing that ye are thereunto called, that ye should inherit a blessing (1 Peter 3:9).

Although many try to explain what this verse means, few are willing to take it at face value. The Christian who goes against the tide of nominal Christianity on this issue and decides to live in this way, immediately becomes a radical in their eyes.

As stated earlier, one of the main reasons we exist is to share the good news of the Gospel with others and to help them to a saving knowledge of Jesus Christ.

If I were the unsaved neighbor of a Christian, how eager would I be to hear him tell me about how the Lord is working in his life, after his lawyer had just sent me a lawsuit document concerning an ongoing property line dispute? Sometimes non-Christians are hardened against Christianity because Christians become involved in such disputes.

Some Christians attempt to make an exception when it comes to serving in the armed forces. They say a Christian, in service to his country, could be within the will of God while killing another human being.

However, in the strictest sense of the word, this is not the Christian's country. Christians ought to respect laws, pray for their leaders, pay taxes, and live as peaceably as possible. But the Christian's real country is a heavenly country. We live temporarily on earth. We are just passing through.

When speaking of Abraham, the writer of the book of Hebrews says this in Hebrews 11:9-10:

> By faith he sojourned in the land of promise, as in a strange country, dwelling in tabernacles with Isaac and Jacob, the heirs with him of the same promise: For he looked for a city which hath foundations, whose builder and maker is God.

Continuing in verses 13-16:

> These all died in faith, not having received the promises, but having seen them afar off, and were per-

> suaded of them, and embraced them, and confessed that they were strangers and pilgrims on the earth. For they that say such things declare plainly that they seek a country. And truly, if they had been mindful of that country from whence they came out, they might have had opportunity to have returned. But now they desire a better country, that is, an heavenly: wherefore God is not ashamed to be called their God: for he hath prepared for them a city.

Jesus, in His conversation with Pilate, said:

> My kingdom is not of this world: if my kingdom were of this world, then would my servants fight, that I should not be delivered to the Jews: but now is my kingdom not from hence (John 18:36).

With Jesus as our leader and example, we take the same position. Our energy and focus is on promoting the Kingdom of God, not on protecting the pride and agenda of an earthly country.

There are accounts of men who profess Christianity, while at the same time being active fighter pilots for the Air Force. To the radical Christian, these two opposites simply are not reconcilable. How, on the one hand, can we follow the mandates of Jesus by loving our enemies, doing good to them which despitefully use us, and sharing the good news of salvation, and on the other hand be willing to send them into eternity without any opportunity to hear the saving gospel of Jesus Christ? Both cannot be right.

This is a weighty doctrine with enormous consequences. Any man who joins an organization which utilizes armed force must reckon that he could die for the cause. A certain percentage of the armed forces never returns alive from combat. Someone has said, "An earthly cause yields an earthly conflict which yields an earthly casualty."

Jesus was teaching His disciples one day, being fully aware that He was about to be captured and crucified. In Luke 22, He directed that if they did not have a sword they should buy one. The disciples found two and Jesus said that would be enough. Two would certainly not have been enough if they were going to use them to resist their enemies. It seems they should have had at least twelve. When Peter did use one to cut off a soldier's ear, he was rebuked by Jesus Who promptly returned the ear and healed the man Peter had struck.

> When they which were about him saw what would follow, they said unto him, Lord, shall we smite with the sword? And one of them smote the servant of the high priest, and cut off his right ear. And Jesus answered and said, Suffer ye thus far. And he touched his ear, and healed him (Luke 22:49-51).

In Matthew's account of the same scene we read these words:

> Then said Jesus unto him, Put up again thy sword into his place: for all they that take the sword shall perish with the sword (Matthew 26:52).

This was a teaching moment for Jesus. Two swords were more than enough if there was no intention to use them for fighting.

Jesus asks for the same commitment today of those who choose to take Him as their "Commander in Chief."

> Then said Jesus unto his disciples, If any man will come after me, let him deny himself, and take up his

> cross, and follow me. For whosoever will save his life shall lose it: and whosoever will lose his life for my sake shall find it (Matthew 16:24-25).

It is impossible to follow the commands of two Commanders in Chief when they run counter to one another. (The term "Chief" itself indicates only one can hold that position for his followers.) One commander or the other at times must be disobeyed.

> No man can serve two masters: for either he will hate the one, and love the other; or else he will hold to the one, and despise the other (Matthew 6:24).

Pride and covetousness are the driving forces of conflict. One person's perceived rights and ambitions come into conflict with another's. Wars upon wars have been fought over the right to control and own property (territories or countries).

> From whence come wars and fightings among you? come they not hence, even of your lusts that war in your members? Ye lust, and have not: ye kill, and desire to have, and cannot obtain: ye fight and war, yet ye have not, because ye ask not. Ye ask, and receive not, because ye ask amiss, that ye may consume it upon your lusts (James 4:1-3).

Within the framework of the radical Christian mindset, saving a neighbor's soul is of higher priority than personal pride or rights. What is the Christian willing to give up for the cause of advancing the Kingdom of God? Shall Christians insist on personal rights at the possible cost of the loss of souls? Shall I, by my prideful insistence on having it my way, cause another to become resistant towards becoming a Christian? God forbid. My goal is to help others understand that Christianity is desirable because it is the only way to receive the gift of eternal life.

Jesus willingly gave up His right to remove Himself from the cross and exact revenge on the ones who nailed Him there. Rather, He offered His life as a gift of salvation to the whole world because He loved every person.

> This is my commandment, That ye love one another, as I have loved you. Greater love hath no man than this, that a man lay down his life for his friends (John 15:12, 13).

The concept of non-resistance or turning the other cheek is very encompassing. It involves every area of interpersonal relationships: marriage, work place, church, community, state, and nation. A radical Christian cannot hold a job that requires use of weapons or arm-twisting to force compliance. This would include security firms, police force, guards at correction facilities, etc. It also includes personal vengeance such as: law suits, restraining orders, liens on property, verbal threats, and other similar acts. Ephesians 6:9 tells Christian masters not to threaten their servants. By the same principle, we are not to threaten our employees or employers.

> Ye masters, do the same things unto them, forbearing threatening: knowing that your Master also is in heaven; neither is there respect of persons with him (Ephesians 6:9).

It is not our duty to see that justice is carried out on the earth. We are rather to be the peaceable ones, showing love and goodwill to all. All wrongs will be made right someday, in God's own timing. Meanwhile, Christians are to love both friend and foe.

> Ye have heard that it hath been said, Thou shalt love thy neighbour, and hate thine enemy. But I say unto you, Love your enemies, bless them that curse you, do good to them that hate you, and pray for them which despitefully use you, and persecute you; That ye may be the children of your Father which is in heaven: for he maketh his sun to rise on the evil and on the good, and sendeth rain on the just and on the unjust. For if ye love them which love you, what reward have ye? do not even the publicans the same? And if ye salute your brethren only, what do ye more than others? do not even the publicans so? Be ye therefore perfect, even as your Father which is in heaven is perfect (Matthew 5:43-48).

> Dearly beloved, avenge not yourselves, but rather give place unto wrath: for it is written, Vengeance is mine; I will repay, saith the Lord (Romans 12:19).

In a serious life-threatening situation, it would be far better for the Christian to die (who is right with God and assured a place of rest) than for the person who is not ready for eternity to die and have a face-to-face meeting with God.

There have been many radical Christians who have died for their faith without resisting rather than waver from the path of Jesus' teaching.

In relating to fellow Christians the entire subject can be reduced to one profound statement found in 1 John 4:20-21.

> If a man say, I love God, and hateth his brother, he is a liar: for he that loveth not his brother whom he hath seen, how can he love God whom he hath not seen? And this commandment have we from him, That he who loveth God love his brother also.

There is no ambiguous theology in this verse, but we attempt to make it difficult because of our human nature. We simply do not want to give everything up for the cause of Christ. Love does not kill, hate, slander, curse, envy, sue, or retaliate.

Christians have not always done well in the area of interpersonal relationships. Churches split and splinter, not always because of doctrinal error, but sometimes because of the inability of "saints" to get along with one another in Christian love.

We cannot change the terms of love; God has defined them. We must ask God to help us overcome our old habits of vindictive aggression to match His standard of love, so that we do not fall short of the grace of God.

Study and Discussion Questions:

1. *The teaching of nonresistance is for whom?*
2. *Can we kill and love simultaneously?*
3. *How are we to treat our worst enemy?*
4. *Can we love God and yet hate our brother?*

Chapter 13
AVOIDING EVIL

-10	-5	0
Idols / Pornography / Sexually Explicit Websites, Books or Films, etc.	|	No Wicked Thing Before My Eyes *Psalm 101:3 Psalm 125:5*

One of the primary marks of a radical Christian is the unwillingness to be involved in sin or even to spend time in presumptuous experimentation of life's gray areas.

Fleshly lusts have a drawing effect on us. Satan has been extremely effective in packaging evil as something to be desired, and presenting that indulging in selfish lusts is acceptable. All are allured toward evil and many failing to avail themselves of the grace of God become ensnared. We must always be on guard and hate evil. It should never feel good to sin!

When we sin, we should despise Satan more for having sold us his package of sin one more time. We should abhor ourselves for failing to avail ourselves of the grace of God. God has clearly stated that He will not send us any temptation that we will not be able to overcome.

> There hath no temptation taken you but such as is common to man: but God is faithful, who will not suffer you to be tempted above that ye are able; but will with the temptation also make a way to escape, that ye may be able to bear it (1 Corinthians 10:13).

To give up and give in to sin sets the stage for regret. If by the grace of God we are able to recover from the sin itself, we will not avoid the law of sowing and reaping. In mercy, God may lessen the extent of reaping when we turn to Him for forgiveness, but the consequences for sin cannot be canceled. If we refuse to turn to God for help and forgiveness, we will without fail enter into spiritual bondage. If we continue in sin, there are no discounts or deals by putting the title of Christian after our name.

> I will behave myself wisely in a perfect way. O when wilt thou come unto me? I will walk within my house with a perfect heart. I will set no wicked thing before mine eyes: I hate the work of them that turn aside; it shall not cleave to me. A froward heart shall depart from me: I will not know a wicked person (Psalm 101:2-4).

> As for such as turn aside unto their crooked ways, the LORD shall lead them forth with the workers of iniquity: but peace shall be upon Israel (Psalm 125:5).

Many professing Christians seemingly have no fear of indulging in pornography, x-rated movies and cheap novels, filthy jokes, or openly lusting after the scantily clad woman on the street. Many times I have heard the statement, "It doesn't matter if you look, as long as you don't touch." Does Satan have us so confused we cannot even understand a simple verse such as Matthew 5:28?

> But I say unto you, That whosoever looketh on a woman to lust after her hath committed adultery with her already in his heart.

It seems that many Christians believe that these behaviors are normal and harmless. Nothing could be farther from the truth. God has set the standard at a Zero position for complete purity. No indulging in evil is acceptable. Immorality is sin. If we engage in such practices, we will pay dearly and severely in loss of spiritual vitality. We cannot serve two masters.

> Finally, brethren, whatsoever things are true, whatsoever things are honest, whatsoever things are just, whatsoever things are pure, whatsoever things are lovely, whatsoever things are of good report; if there be any virtue, and if there be any praise, think on these things (Philippians 4:8).

Why does it matter to God what we watch or read or think upon? Because we cannot remain unaffected by what we take in; consequently, what goes in must come out. No fountain can send forth both bitter water and sweet.

> Out of the same mouth proceedeth blessing and cursing. My brethren, these things ought not so to be.

> Doth a fountain send forth at the same place sweet water and bitter? Can the fig tree, my brethren, bear olive berries? either a vine, figs? so can no fountain both yield salt water and fresh (James 3:10-12).

We cannot immerse ourselves in the lust of the world and expect to have close communion with God. We cannot commit lust and adultery in our heart six days a week and then enjoy a wonderful experience with God on Sunday.

> What concord hath Christ with Belial? or what part hath he that believeth with an infidel? And what agreement hath the temple of God with idols? for ye are the temple of the living God; as God hath said, I will dwell in them, and walk in them; and I will be their God, and they shall be my people. Wherefore come out from among them, and be ye separate, saith the Lord, and touch not the unclean thing; and I will receive you, and will be a Father unto you, and ye shall be my sons and daughters, saith the Lord Almighty (2 Corinthians 6:15-18).

The Bible clearly condemns the position of people who claim that God is their Father and that Jesus has saved them, yet they make no attempt to be pure in heart.

The promise of God to receive us and be a father to us is reliant on three requisites:

1. Come out from among those who worship the things of the flesh,
2. Be separate from them in conduct and thought, and
3. Touch not the unclean thing.

What are the unclean things? Unclean things are those things that stain our spiritual purity. In the scriptures we have various lists of things that will separate us from God and His holiness.

> Put to death your members which are on the earth: fornication, uncleanness, passion, evil desire, and covetousness, which is idolatry. Because of these things the wrath of God is coming upon the sons of disobedience (Colossians 3:5-6 NKJV).

How well we know the myriad ways Satan tempts Christians to fall into lust. There are many suggestive things that trigger our imaginations: improperly dressed individuals, smutty stories, books, magazines, advertisements, billboards, etc. We should never underestimate the creativity of the prince of the power of darkness. His great desire is to get Christians out of relationship with God. He will stoop to any method to get a Christian to sin.

The only means of deliverance from impurity is a close walk with God Who gives us the desire to live pure and holy lives. This coupled with Holy Spirit power sustains and gives us the ability to live near the standard of Holiness to which we are called. There is no way to live pure holy lives in our own strength.

Without reading the Word of God, we cannot know the standard of holy living. Apart from the Word of God every man does what is right in his own eyes. Without a standard or Zero position, there is no knowledge of the horrible sinfulness of sin. However, God has set a standard. Whether we know about it or not, His is still the standard by which we shall be judged.

Just as ignorance of the tax laws does not make us exempt from payment of taxes, so it is with God's laws. The standard is found in His Word. Either we conform to His standard and live, or we choose rebellion and face eternal death.

Study and Discussion Questions:

1. *Lust is an evil desire. Where does it come from?*
2. *What is holiness?*
3. *How do we become holy?*
4. *Can we see Jesus in unholiness?*
5. *Can a person plead ignorance?*

Chapter 14
HEADSHIP ORDER

-10	-5	0
Uncovered Head / Cut Hair	|	The Christian Woman's Headship Veiling *1Corinthians 11:5, 6*

To the casual observer, the most visible sign of the doctrine of Divine Headship Order is the covered head of the woman. This object: the prayer veiling, also called a covering, headship veiling, and prayer cap, is an item that causes eyebrows to be raised and questions to be asked. But this is a New Testament doctrine everyone needs to understand.

As was stated earlier, God is a God of order. First in the Old Testament and later in the New Testament, God set up lines of authority. Immediately after Adam and Eve fell, God pronounced judgment on all the parties involved (Satan, Eve, and Adam). Notice what He said to Eve.

> I will greatly multiply thy sorrow and thy conception; in sorrow thou shalt bring forth children; and thy desire shall be to thy husband, and he shall rule over thee (Genesis 3:16).

God created the female (woman, Eve) for a help meet (companion: suitable helper) for the male (man, Adam). Each was created for a special purpose, different but yet 100% complimentary. Before the fall, there was no pride-driven desire to escape God-given positions in life. Before the man and woman transgressed, found in Genesis 3, God elected to establish the line of authority. This is a foundational principle, founded years before Abraham or the Law of Moses. Eve was to be Adam's helper. He was to be her head (leader of the relationship).

Since we live in the New Testament era, the New Testament applies to us as believers. God spells out the headship order simply in 1 Corinthians 11:3. Again, this is clear, plain language, not hard to understand if we really want to know God's position on the matter.

> I would have you know, that the head of every man is Christ; and the head of the woman is the man; and the head of Christ is God (1 Corinthians 11:3).

The divine order in the home is; God, Christ, man, woman, children. The husband, under Christ, is to oversee the home. The wife at his side is to support and undergird him. The children are to obey their parents.

In our society, with everybody wanting to do their own thing, this commandment is taken quite lightly and often ignored. Many think, *It is a good idea. It probably is ideal, but it doesn't seem possible for our family.*

God blesses obedience, regardless of whether society promotes women's lib, self-expression, empowerment, and women in authority over men. God only puts His blessing on obedience. Secular ideas of ideal marriages, home life, and lines of authority, when not founded on the Zero position as found in God' s Word, will not bring God's richest blessing to the home regardless of how reasonable they sound.

Sometimes women blame the inequality of the sexes as a plot to suppress women and to keep them from experiencing their full potential. These women ignore God's Word on the subject. A woman is to find her fulfillment in obedience to the Word of God and this means being subject to her husband. Any woman who is fulfilling her place in God's order is not a second-rate citizen, nor are they unfulfilled. How can a Christian woman be unfulfilled while abiding in God's will?

A large portion of the responsibility for the horrible state of affairs in this nation can be laid at the feet of the breakdown of the home and family. There are dysfunctional marriages and families on every hand. God is not revered as the Head over all and Jesus the Head of man.

Many men, because of selfishness or ignorance, have not taken their God-given responsibilities as heads of their homes under Christ. Many women, because of pride or ignorance, have failed to take their God-given places under the headship of their husbands. All men and women since Adam and Eve have a heart of pride that wishes to do what they want to do when they want to do it.

This does not line up with the Biblical teaching; therefore, radical Christianity does not accept this selfish lifestyle as an option.

This same concept of women being in submission is also to be observed within the church setting.

> Let your women keep silence in the churches: for it is not permitted unto them to speak; but they are commanded to be under obedience, as also saith the law. And if they will learn any thing, let them ask their husbands at home: for it is a shame for women to speak in the church (1 Corinthians 14:34-35).

This passage does not mean that a woman cannot open her mouth in the house of God, but rather that they should not teach men or exercise authority over them. They may sing, give testimony, teach children's classes, and teach women's' classes. Another scripture states that the older women should teach the younger women. There is more than enough for the sisters to do in the church setting.

> The aged women likewise, that they be in behavior as becometh holiness, not false accusers, not given to much wine, teachers of good things; that they may teach the young women to be sober, to love their husbands, to love their children, to be discreet, chaste, keepers at home, good, obedient to their own husbands, that the word of God be not blasphemed (Titus 2:3-5).

There are Christian churches that allow or even encourage women to serve as pastors. The Scripture is very plain that women are not to hold this office in the Christian church. Women are not totally to blame, however. Men, in direct opposition to Bible directives regarding how a Christian church is to function, have through neglect and laziness given up their God-given responsibility and have allowed women of the church to do work that was given to the male. Radical Christians do not believe that women are unspiritual, incapable speakers, imperceptive, or should have no role in church life. Men are to follow their Head which is Christ. He has spoken.

> I suffer not a woman to teach, nor to usurp authority over the man, but to be in silence. For Adam was first formed, then Eve. And Adam was not deceived, but the woman being deceived was in the transgression (1 Timothy 2:12-14).

How does the woman's headship veiling fit into the Divine Headship Order? The passage that introduces this ordinance is found in the eleventh chapter of First Corinthians.

> I want you to know that the head of every man is Christ, the head of woman is man, and the head of Christ is God. Every man praying or prophesying, having his head covered, dishonors his head. But every woman who prays or prophesies with her head uncovered dishonors her head, for that is one and the same as if her head were shaved. For if a woman is not covered, let her also be shorn. But if it is shameful for a woman to be shorn or shaved, let her be covered. For a man indeed ought not to cover his head, since he is the image and glory of God; but woman is the glory of man. For man is not from woman, but woman from man. Nor was man created for the woman, but wom-

> an for the man. For this reason the woman ought to have a symbol of authority on her head, because of the angels (1 Corinthians 11:3-10 NKJV).

The badge of a police officer is the symbol of authority. It is a symbol of the right he has to uphold the law within his jurisdiction. The badge portrays that he is operating under the authority of the law of the municipality and that the local government will support him as he makes an arrest. The badge in itself gives no rights, but is a token of the authority vested in him. In most municipalities, an officer is required to have his badge in his possession while operating in his official capacity as an identification of his position. Those who see it know that he exercises his authority under that of the municipality in which he operates.

When a man has his hair cut short and his head uncovered while praying, he honors God, his authority. A woman who has long hair and has her head covered while praying, honors God and her husband, her authority. By their obedience, both are giving assent to the fact that they are in agreement with and wish to be under the authority and blessing of their head, Jesus Christ.

Today, in many circles there is still a stigma attached to a woman's shaved head or very short hair. When we see a woman with a shaved head, we question what message she is trying to portray. Perhaps it is done for shock value or may be a signal that she will not bow to the God-given role of women.

Even though long hair on men is somewhat more accepted, there is still a stigma attached. It certainly sends a signal that they wish to identify with the counter culture. It is quite doubtful that a candidate for president of the United States could gather sufficient support to be elected while wearing his hair to his shoulders.

A number of years ago a young man regularly brought electric motors to my shop for repair. He was the son of the owner of a successful business. He was unkempt and wore shoulder length hair with a beard and seemed quite disdainful of convention. His dad always dressed well and wore a suit. One day his dad suddenly passed away, and the son became the heir to the business. A few weeks later, someone whom I did not recognize brought electric motors to the shop for repair. Only when he began to speak did I realize that this was the son. Nice clothes, short hair, no beard, and a much more professional demeanor. Why the sudden change? I believe he realized the professional world would not take him seriously otherwise.

The veiled hair for the women is their badge of authority. It is a sign to the angels and all who are looking on that they are and wish to be under God's authority.

Jesus the Son of God always did the will of His Father, therefore He had all the authority of the Father. When He told the demons to flee, they fled. When He told the wind to become still, the wind became still. When He told the leper to be healed, the leper was healed. He had the authority to do this because He was in perfect harmony with the Father.

The centurion in Matthew 8 understood this. He told Jesus, "You don't have to come to my house, just say the word and my servant will be healed. I understand your authority; I too, am under authority and have the backing of Rome when I make a command. I understand the concept. I know You have all the authority of heaven. When You command my servant to be healed, You do not have to be there to make sure it is done."

> When Jesus had entered Capernaum, a centurion came to Him, pleading with Him, saying, "Lord, my servant is lying at home paralyzed, dreadfully tormented." And Jesus said to him, "I will come and heal him." The centurion answered and said, "Lord, I am not worthy that You should come under my roof. But only speak a word, and my servant will be healed. For I also am a man under authority, having soldiers under me. And I say to this one, 'Go' and he goes; and to another, 'Come,' and he comes; and to my servant, 'Do this', and he does it." When Jesus heard it, He marveled, and said to those who followed, Assuredly, I say to you, I have not found such great faith, not even in Israel! (Matthew 8:5-10 NKJV)

Consequently, by coming under authority, a man or woman of God has the power of heaven at his or her disposal. A woman under authority has power to call down grace and blessing upon her children and herself, even if her husband has not taken his place as the head of the home. The woman who takes her own way and embraces secular methods to attempt to force her husband to be the man he should be will not experience enablement from God.

Many women, doing it God's way, have raised families of God-serving children. They have honored their husbands as their head, even though their husbands did not take their place as spiritual leaders in the home. There is simply no way to improve upon

God's Zero position on this subject. We can rationalize our actions, read self-help books, go to seminars, or join a support group, but if that group, book, or seminar does not uphold God's position on the subject, it is an exercise in futility. It will be neither the right way nor the best way to get relief from the situation. God never said that the right way would be the easiest or most rational, but God always honors obedience.

A Christian home should be a safe house from the storm, a refuge from the debauchery and evil that is on every hand. It is to be a greenhouse that protects and shelters the lives of our children. It is a place to teach by word and example God's truth to the next generation. Our generation will not always be here. We must pass on the pure gospel of Jesus Christ to the next generation or it will be lost. We must not merely pass on a way of life, but rather a spiritual legacy in Jesus Christ Who has brought us everlasting life.

> Jesus saith unto him, I am the way, the truth, and the life: no man cometh unto the Father, but by me (John 14:6).

Any way that compromises the way of Jesus and goes in some other direction is headed for destruction. We are under obligation to preach the gospel simply, honestly, and in its entirety. Any person, minister or otherwise, who dilutes the gospel and deviates from its purity will be held accountable. Paul told the Galatians:

> As we said before, so say I now again, If any man preach any other gospel unto you than that ye have received, let him be accursed (Galatians 1:9).

As men and women under authority, we have an awesome task and responsibility to the next generation. The Lord is able to give us grace to embrace the right and refute the wrong.

Study and Discussion Questions:

1. *For what purpose did God create woman?*
2. *What were the consequences of Eve's and Adam's sin? Name them.*
3. *What is the order in which God identified authority in our lives?*
4. *What are the strengths for the woman's headship veiling?*
5. *Who is the head over all?*
6. *Can we ignore God and still be accepted of Him?*

Chapter 15
ONE MAN AND ONE WOMAN FOR LIFE

-10	-5	0
Divorce / Remarriage	|	One Man / One Woman / Life
Homosexuality / Fornication		*Mark 10:6-12 Romans 1:26-27*

God created man in His own image and quite complex when compared to any other life form on earth. Man was created with spiritual, emotional, and social needs that are absent in the rest of creation. At creation, a perfect spiritual, emotional, and social relationship existed between God and Adam, God and Eve, and Adam and Eve. What followed changed all that. Satan tempted Eve with a lie and she sinned. Adam joined her in eating of the forbidden fruit. Their relationship with God was broken, and the relationship between Adam and Eve was affected.

From the beginning, God stated that when a couple marries, a man should leave his father and mother and cleave to his wife.

> Therefore shall a man leave his father and his mother, and shall cleave unto his wife: and they shall be one flesh (Genesis 2:24).

Immediately after the creation of Eve in Genesis 2, God gave the guidelines for a legitimate sexual relationship. It is not at all complicated, one man and one woman in marriage for life. This statement establishes God's Zero position. This is God's created plan to have our sexual desires met. This cannot be improved upon.

The word marriage is implied but not stated in this passage. In Genesis 3, the words husband and wife are used as God dealt with the guilty pair.

Mark 10 indicates that marriage to an original partner is expected to be the vehicle to physical fulfillment. Anything otherwise is a sinful relationship and cannot be blessed by God.

> From the beginning of the creation God made them male and female. For this cause shall a man leave his father and mother, and cleave to his wife; And they twain shall be one flesh: so then they are no more twain, but one flesh. What therefore God hath joined together, let not man put asunder. And in the house his disciples asked him again of the same matter. And he saith unto them, Whosoever shall put away his wife, and marry another, committeth adultery against her. And if a woman shall put away her

> husband, and be married to another, she committeth adultery (Mark 10:6-12).

God's guidelines concerning marriage apply to every age and culture. However, for every legitimate relationship Satan has created counterfeits and presents them as alternatives for sexual fulfillment. Thus we have adultery, fornication, homosexuality, pornography, pedophilia, and many deviant sexual behaviors and inventions too disgraceful to mention.

Although the sins listed above are actions, they are the result of a breakdown of morals in the heart. The physical act of sin is a manifestation of the evil condition of the heart.

As late as the 1950's, it was shameful to have a child born out of wedlock. Satan has managed to break down the moral fiber of society to the extent that our culture now does not even flinch at unmarried parents, significant others, single parent homes (resulting from immorality) and every other deviation from the Zero position. The society that accommodates same-sex marriage, live-in relationships, and free love is destined to receive God's judgment.

God's Zero position is clear on the matter, regardless of attempts to obscure the truth of God's Word. It is impossible to find favor in God's sight as a saved and sanctified Christian while at the same time being involved in one or more of these diversions. A spring cannot bring forth both salt water and sweet.

> What agreement hath the temple of God with idols? for ye are the temple of the living God; as God hath said, I will dwell in them, and walk in them;

> and I will be their God, and they shall be my people. Wherefore come out from among them, and be ye separate, saith the Lord, and touch not the unclean thing; and I will receive you, And will be a Father unto you, and ye shall be my sons and daughters, saith the Lord Almighty (2 Corinthians 6:16-18).

A man or woman who professes to be the temple of God cannot remain in a deviant sexual relationship which God judges as sin and still be a pure, undefiled child of God. They are not coming out from among the ungodly, nor keeping themselves unspotted from the world. We cannot have it both ways.

Not long ago marriage was sacred to the point that there were forced marriages (shotgun weddings) when it was found that a girl was expecting a child and she and the father were not married. Because he had done her wrong, he was expected to do what he could to make it right by marrying her and supporting both her and the child. Even if the couple did not have the moral inclination themselves to do what was right, the parents saw to it that they married.

A quote from the New York Times, February 2012: "It used to be called illegitimacy. Now it is the new normal. After steadily rising for five decades, the share of children born to unmarried women has crossed a threshold: more than half of births to American women under 30 occur outside marriage."

This does not include abortion statistics. In January 2011, the Guttmacher Institute reported 1.21 million abortions in the US in 2008. Mothers who had abortions now have daughters who are having abortions. The killing of human life continues unabated. Society is increasingly accepting as normal this slaughter of unborn children.

All this comes about by an attempt for sexual pleasure and satisfaction without the attending responsibility. By God's standard, this activity is not normal and will never be normal. They who believe that such selfish and evil behavior can continue without immediate detrimental effects on society or impending judgment are only fooling themselves.

> Be not deceived; God is not mocked: for whatsoever a man soweth, that shall he also reap. For he that soweth to his flesh shall of the flesh reap corruption; but he that soweth to the Spirit shall of the Spirit reap life everlasting (Galatians 6:7-8).

Regardless of how tightly bound a person may be in an ungodly relationship, it is imperative that the relationship be dissolved to secure assurance of salvation. It is unfortunate and heartrending, but according to the Scripture there is no other way.

Modern society has fallen a long way from God's standard. The fabric of morality that invites God's blessing upon a nation is being torn to shreds and, consequently, this nation will continue to reap the dreadful results of moral failure unless she turns to God in repentance.

Study and Discussion Questions:

1. *Who made a man and woman joined in marriage one?*
2. *Does God call adultery sin because it is an act? What about the marriage itself?*
3. *How many abortions were performed in 2008? How many would that make in 10 years? 50 years? 100 years?*
4. *Of what do we reap?*

Chapter 16
THE DAY OF REST

I have already stated that the Day of Rest was a Creation principle. The seven-day week is established in Genesis 1 through chapter 2:2. The concept of the Day of Rest as a Sabbath Day is first introduced in Genesis 2: 3:

> And God blessed the seventh day, and sanctified it: because that in it he had rested from all his work which God created and made.

God included the observance of the Sabbath in the Ten Commandments. From the beginning of the world God required and expected a day of sanctification and worship.

> Remember the Sabbath day, to keep it holy. Six days shalt thou labour, and do all thy work: But the seventh day is the sabbath of the LORD thy God: in it thou shalt not do any work, thou, nor thy son, nor

> thy daughter, thy manservant, nor thy maidservant, nor thy cattle, nor thy stranger that is within thy gates: For in six days the LORD made heaven and earth, the sea, and all that in them is, and rested the seventh day: wherefore the LORD blessed the sabbath day, and hallowed it (Exodus 20:8-11).

This special day of rest was not given only to the Hebrew people but was to be a universally observed day, ordained since creation week.

We here have an account of the original institution of the day of rest. Like the institution of marriage, it was given to man for the whole race. Those who worshipped God seemed to have kept the Sabbath from the first, and there are tokens of this in the brief sketch the Bible contains of the ages before the giving of the law at Mount Sinai. Noah sent forth the raven from the ark, and the dove thrice, at intervals of seven days, Genesis 8:1-22. The account of the sending of manna in the desert proves that the Sabbath was already known and observed, Exodus 16:22-30. The week was an established division of time in Mesopotamia and Arabia, Genesis 29:27; and traces of it have been found in many nations of antiquity, so remote from each other and of such diverse origin as to forbid the idea of their having received it from Sinai and the Hebrews.

American Tract Society Bible Dictionary

> The purpose of the Sabbath was to be a holy intermission. The Sabbath was a command to be observed for rest and remembrance.

> The seventh day is the Sabbath of the LORD thy God: in it thou shalt not do any work, thou, nor thy son, nor thy daughter, nor thy manservant, nor thy maidservant, nor thine ox, nor thine ass, nor any of thy cattle, nor thy stranger that is within thy gates; that thy manservant and thy maidservant may rest as well as thou. And remember that thou wast a servant in the land of Egypt, and that the LORD thy God brought thee out thence through a mighty hand and by a stretched out arm: therefore the LORD thy God commanded thee to keep the Sabbath day (Deuteronomy 5:14-15).

The concept has not changed. We still need one day out of seven to rest and worship. And, because we all forget, we need to be reminded of the deliverance from sins that God has granted to those who have trusted Jesus Christ for cleansing through His shed blood.

The Children of Israel in the Old Testament had many external rules and rituals that governed their lives. There we have an account of a man that gathered sticks on the Sabbath whose punishment was by stoning (Numbers 15:32-36). It may seem somewhat harsh, but it was necessary to impress on those present the seriousness of disobedience to God's eternal precepts. However, observing the day merely out of duty but not with the spirit, has always been a problem with mankind.

> To what purpose is the multitude of your sacrifices unto me? saith the LORD: I am full of the burnt offerings of rams, and the fat of fed beasts; and I de-

> light not in the blood of bullocks, or of lambs, or of he goats. When ye come to appear before me, who hath required this at your hand, to tread my courts? Bring no more vain oblations; incense is an abomination unto me; the new moons and sabbaths, the calling of assemblies, I cannot away with; it is iniquity, even the solemn meeting. Your new moons and your appointed feasts my soul hateth: they are a trouble unto me; I am weary to bear them. And when ye spread forth your hands, I will hide mine eyes from you: yea, when ye make many prayers, I will not hear: your hands are full of blood.
>
> Wash you, make you clean; put away the evil of your doings from before mine eyes; cease to do evil; learn to do well; seek judgment, relieve the oppressed, judge the fatherless, plead for the widow (Isaiah 1:11-17).

Those who have attended church from their childhood have sometimes done so with less than pure motives. Maybe we attended because of habit or fear of what others might think if we would not have attended. Although such attendance may be better than not attending, we miss the full blessing of true, collective worship of the Lord.

Jesus told the woman at the well that the place of worship would no longer be important. It is more important to worship with a true heart filled with the Holy Spirit. Any worship of God that does not include these two aspects is a farce and an affront to God.

> The sacrifice of the wicked is an abomination to the LORD: but the prayer of the upright is his delight (Proverbs 15:8).

> Keep thy foot when thou goest to the house of God, and be more ready to hear, than to give the sacrifice of fools: for they consider not that they do evil (Ecclesiastes 5:1).

We notice in the New Testament church a change from Sabbath/Saturday to Lord's day/Sunday. First we must recognize that there was no command to change the day. However, there are a number of reasons why we believe it was moved to the first day of the week.

1. Sunday worship commemorates the resurrection of Jesus which took place on the first day of the week.

2. It was on Sunday that Jesus appeared to His apostles on at least one occasion.

> The same day at evening, being the first day of the week, when the doors were shut where the disciples were assembled for fear of the Jews, came Jesus and stood in the midst, and saith unto them, Peace be unto you (John 20:19).

3. As New Testament Christians, we willingly offer the Lord the first day of our week, also called The Lord's Day, or Sunday as we know it, which became the regular day of worship in the early apostolic church.

> Upon the first day of the week, when the disciples came together to break bread, Paul preached unto them, ready to depart on the morrow; and continued his speech until midnight (Acts 20:7).

> Upon the first day of the week let every one of you lay by him in store, as God hath prospered him, that there be no gatherings when I come (1 Corinthians 16:2).

In the years after Christ, the Christians' custom of meeting on Sunday was so well known that an ordinary test question put by persecutors to those suspected of Christianity was, "Hast thou kept the Lord's day?" The Christian's reply was, "I am a Christian; I cannot omit it."

About A.D. 160, Justin Martyr observed that

> On the day called Sunday, all who live in cities or in the country gather together to one place, and the memoirs of the apostles or writings of the prophets are read .... But Sunday is the day on which we all hold our common assembly, because it is the first day on which God ... made the world. And Jesus Christ our Savior rose from the dead on that same day.*

How has New Testament worship changed from Old Testament worship? Old Testament worship included many external rituals. It included trumpets, stringed instruments, temple choirs, commanded rituals, blood sacrifices, incense smoke, gold, purple, fine linen, brass, elaborate garments for the High Priest, beautiful

---

*Bercot, David W. A Dictionary of Early Christian Beliefs: A Reference Guide to More Than 700 Topics Discussed by the Early Church Fathers, 1998, pp. 405, 406.

temples, etc. The requirement for New Testament worship is "in spirit and in truth"--truth about one's position in relation to God, in relation to His Word, and in relation to others. It doesn't appear that the first century church had many rules about conduct on the Lord's Day. They relied more on the spirit of the Law. Justin Martyr 100-165 AD (early Christian) wrote:

> The ordinary business of life is to be wholly laid aside, both for the sake of bodily and mental health, and chiefly to secure the quiet and uninterrupted employment of the sacred hours for religious purposes. The spirit of the law clearly forbids all uses of the day which are worldly, such as amusements, journeys, etc., whereby one fails to keep the day holy himself, or hinders others in doing so.

When the Old Testament people's hearts were not turned toward God, the Laws of God were meaningless in their daily lives. Although the Law condemned their actions and they were punished for their transgressions, they did not discontinue their disobedience. Jeremiah told of a day when obedience to the law, instead of pressing from the outside in, would flow from the inside out.

> This shall be the covenant that I will make with the house of Israel; After those days, saith the LORD, I will put my law in their inward parts, and write it in their hearts; and will be their God, and they shall be my people (Jeremiah 31:33).

In the New Testament believer, through the Holy Spirit, the Ark of the Covenant has been moved from an external position to an internal place in the heart. However, if this transfer has never taken place in our lives, the New Testament principles of Lord's Day observance will not mean one bit more to us than did the Old Testament laws to the disobedient Jews.

If New Testament Christians do not believe that the Lord's Day was given for a blessing, for the spreading of the Gospel, and for a holy intermission to bless man, then of course it becomes a chore. Obedience to a day of holy intermission hinders these worldly believers from making money or pursuing pleasure on the Lord's Day. It cramps their selfish lifestyle.

To the radical Christian, the Lord's Day is received with thanksgiving as a gift from the hand of Almighty God. The Lord's Day is a thoughtful gesture from God to us, deferring to our fragile nature. He knows all our thoughts and feelings of weariness, so He gives us the blessing of a holy intermission for rejuvenation and reflection. Praise God.

How do we then get the most blessing from this gift? The ordinary business of life includes things like buying, selling, working at your occupation, canning, cooking, sewing, washing, shopping, running errands, cleaning, repairing, eating out, gardening, financial decision making, building, strategizing, plotting and planning, work without end. As much as possible, these things must be laid aside to give ourselves to the rejuvenating of body and spirit. If we engage in the same things we do every work day, the Day of Rest fails to become a holy intermission.

What are some activities that are good and right on the Lord's Day?

1. Go to a house of worship. Meet and worship with other believers.

2. Give encouragement to others by visiting, writing, calling, or e-mailing.

3. Visit shut-ins or the elderly.

4. Bible reading.

5. Read books that exemplify the Christian life. Read about what is happening in the missions that your church supports.

6. Play with your children; take them on a picnic after church.

7. Research Bible doctrine.

There is no end of good things that can be done to make the Lord's Day a meaningful intermission.

What about the exceptions? We do live in the day of grace, and there are things that come up which do not neatly fit into the mold of being definitely right or wrong on the Lord's Day. So we must check our motives and compare them to the spirit of the law.

The Lord's Day was made for man, not the other way around. Jesus said that it is lawful to do good on the Sabbath. If a neighbor's house is burning at 6:00 on a Sunday morning, we should want to be there to help do what we can to alleviate the problem.

Christians ought not to use the "day of grace" excuse, or the "Christian liberties" excuse for shortcomings in proper planning for the "Holy Intermission." If something important is forgotten, rather than going out and buying it on the Lord's Day, try to do without it. It may help us to remember in the future.

God has given this principle for our blessing. The way to reap the blessing is obedience. There is no substitute for keeping the Spirit of the Law.

Study and Discussion Questions:

1. *Who established the day of rest and why?*
2. *Was there an established day of rest before the Mosaic Law was given?*
3. *What are the evidences that the early New Testament church practiced keeping a day of rest?*
4. *When did the church come together for worship?*
5. *What is the meaning of Jesus' words; "the Sabbath was made for man and not man for the Sabbath?"*

Chapter 17
CHURCH AND STATE

Many Christians do not want the government to tell them how to run their church, but they are more than willing to tell the government how to operate. One of the defining characteristics of a radical Biblicist is his literal interpretation that the Kingdom of Jesus Christ is separate from the kingdoms of this world. A major pillar upon which this position is built comes from Jesus' answer to Pilate at His trial.

> Jesus answered, My kingdom is not of this world: if my kingdom were of this world, then would my servants fight, that I should not be delivered to the Jews: but now is my kingdom not from hence (John 18:36).

Jesus admitted to being a king, but reassured Pilate that He was not trying to take his job. Consequently, Pilate told the Jews that he found no fault in Jesus.

Jesus prayed thus to the Father:

> I have given them thy word; and the world hath hated them, because they are not of the world, even as I am not of the world. I pray not that thou shouldest take them out of the world, but that thou shouldest keep them from the evil. They are not of the world, even as I am not of the world (John 17:14-16).

By spiritual birth, Christians are citizens of Heaven, though by natural birth they hold an earthly citizenship.

> These all [Abel, Enoch, Noah, Abraham, Sara] died in faith, not having received the promises, but having seen them afar off, and were persuaded of them, and embraced them, and confessed that they were strangers and pilgrims on the earth. For they that say such things declare plainly that they seek a country. And truly, if they had been mindful of that country from whence they came out, they might have had opportunity to have returned. But now they desire a better country, that is, an heavenly: wherefore God is not ashamed to be called their God: for he hath prepared for them a city (Hebrews 11:13-16).

As citizens of another country, yet still on this earth, we are in the position of an ambassador. Paul in his writings twice refers to the concept that we are ambassadors.

> We are ambassadors for Christ, as though God did beseech you by us: we pray you in Christ's stead, be ye reconciled to God (2 Corinthians 5:20).

> I am an ambassador in bonds: that therein I may speak boldly, as I ought to speak (Ephesians 6:20).

Ambassador: the highest-ranking diplomatic representative appointed by a country or government to represent it in another.

This describes the Christian. We represent the heavenly kingdom. We have pledged our allegiance to Christ Who is King. We are called to live before this world the values of the heavenly kingdom. Of us, those of the kingdom's of this world query about Christ and His kingdom. What quality of ambassadors are we? Are we true representatives of citizens of the heavenly kingdom?

We live and do business here. We hold physical jobs, buy supplies, and use this world's services. We use their hospitals and are protected by their police. We pay taxes and obey all the laws we can without violating the laws of our heavenly kingdom.

The heavenly kingdom offers goods and services superior to anything found on earth. We are to promote these goods and services to the citizens of this world. The heavenly kingdom offers eternal life, peace and joy, love and goodwill, the indwelling of the Holy Spirit, and a retirement community that is the best.

Heavenly goods and services are not available in this world's markets at any price. There are cheap imitations and counterfeits readily available, but all good and perfect things have to be imported.

> Every good gift and every perfect gift is from above, and cometh down from the Father of lights, with whom is no variableness, neither shadow of turning (James 1:17).

Our spiritual food must be sent from our home country, for any spiritual food we pick up locally is tainted with sin and the water is contaminated.

We, as ambassadors of heaven, are not to fight the wars of the nations of this world. We are not to vote in their elections, play their games, listen to their music, drink their wine, or watch their movies. We have a higher calling, and that is to represent the heavenly kingdom to the masses of this world, in every area of life.

> Love not the world, neither the things that are in the world. If any man love the world, the love of the Father is not in him (1 John 2:15).

An embassy building is a little world of its own operating within another country. For the embassy to have a viable presence in the country, all personnel must be part of a united front. The entire embassy staff works for the good of the country that it represents. No one can be doing projects on their own, and not be responsible to the head of the embassy.

Even though it is on foreign soil, the embassy is run and protected by the laws of the country it represents. The U.S. military protects the U.S embassies. The security of each person is connected to the fact that the embassy knows each person's duties and can send protection with them wherever they go. If, in fact, an ambassador is in a country hostile to the ideals of his home country, then he will be grateful for the protection available to him. If he slips out without notifying security, they cannot be responsible for his protection; he is on his own.

Likewise, the Church, the embassy of the heavenly kingdom,

is to function according to heavenly mandates and doctrines. It is being protected by heaven's army. The church is to operate as a unified embassy.

All Christians are under the authority of Jesus Christ, Ruler of the heavenly kingdom. We take directions from the Head, faithfully dispatching the duties given to us. We are responsible for one another. We care for each other, and we are concerned about how each one is doing. Are others receiving the supplies and support they need to do their job properly? Are we getting too cozy with our host country? Are we losing personnel to the world and its allure? Have we lost our sense of obligation to represent our country and allegiance to our Head?

What responsibilities do we assume when we become ambassadors for the heavenly kingdom? What is expected?

1. WE OFFER UNDYING ALLEGIANCE TO JESUS AND HIS KINGDOM.

> Love not the world, neither the things that are in the world. If any man love the world, the love of the Father is not in him (1 John 2:15).

Demas, a companion of the apostle Paul, failed in this.

> Demas hath forsaken me, having loved this present world, and is departed unto Thessalonica (2 Timothy 4:10).

2. WE USE PERSONAL TALENTS AND RESOURCES FOR JESUS AND HIS KINGDOM.

> He gave some, apostles; and some, prophets; and some, evangelists; and some, pastors and teachers; for

> the perfecting of the saints, for the work of the ministry, for the edifying of the body of Christ (Ephesians 4:11-12).

Whether God has given each man one talent or ten talents, they are to be used for building the church. God did not bless us with skills and abilities to be wasted on our own desires and lusts, but rather to invest them in kingdom work: teaching, singing, doing mission work, praying, etc.

> The kingdom of heaven is as a man travelling into a far country, who called his own servants, and delivered unto them his goods. And unto one he gave five talents, to another two, and to another one; to every man according to his several ability; and straightway took his journey (Matthew 25:14-15).

3. WE REPRESENT JESUS AND HIS KINGDOM TO OUR HOST COUNTRY.

Christian ambassadors have a superior King, Who offers a superior life, superior gifts, and a superior future. All the advantages far out-weigh the disadvantages. The advantages of the Christian's home country, heaven, ought to be proclaimed. In fact, Christians are commanded to promote Jesus and His kingdom.

> Ye shall receive power, after that the Holy Ghost is come upon you: and ye shall be witnesses unto me both in Jerusalem, and in all Judaea, and in Samaria, and unto the uttermost part of the earth. Amen (Acts 1:8).

We also have obligations concerning the nations of this world even though this is not where our spiritual citizenship lies.

1. CHRISTIANS ARE TO PRAY FOR THEIR CIVIL RULERS.

> I exhort therefore, that, first of all, supplications, prayers, intercessions, and giving of thanks, be made for all men; for kings, and for all that are in authority; that we may lead a quiet and peaceable life in all godliness and honesty (1 Timothy 2:1-2).

2. WE ARE TO OBEY THE GOVERNMENT IN EVERY AREA WE CAN.

> Put them in mind to be subject to principalities and powers, to obey magistrates, to be ready to every good work (Titus 3:1).

> Submit yourselves to every ordinance of man for the Lord's sake: whether it be to the king, as supreme; or unto governors, as unto them that are sent by him for the punishment of evildoers, and for the praise of them that do well (1 Peter 2:13-14).

3. CHRISTIANS ARE TAUGHT TO PAY TAXES.

> For this cause pay ye tribute also: for they are God's ministers, attending continually upon this very thing (Romans 13:6).

> Show me a penny. Whose image and superscription hath it? They answered and said, Caesar's.

And he said unto them, Render therefore unto Caesar the things which be Caesar's, and unto God the things which be God's (Luke 20:24-25).

4. WE ARE TO HONOR THE RULERS IN AUTHORITY.

Render therefore to all their dues: tribute to whom tribute is due; custom to whom custom; fear to whom fear; honor to whom honor (Romans 13:7).

5. CHRISTIANS ARE TO BE THE ILLUMINATING LIGHT AND PRESERVING SALT OF THE NATION IN WHICH THEY LIVE.

Ye are the salt of the earth: but if the salt have lost his savour, wherewith shall it be salted? it is thenceforth good for nothing, but to be cast out, and to be trodden under foot of men.

Ye are the light of the world. A city that is set on an hill cannot be hid. Neither do men light a candle, and put it under a bushel, but on a candlestick; and it giveth light unto all that are in the house. Let your light so shine before men, that they may see your good works, and glorify your Father which is in heaven (Matthew 5:13-16).

THIS WORLD IS NOT MY HOME

This world is not my home; I'm just passing through.
My treasures are laid up somewhere beyond the blue.
The angels beckon me from Heaven's open door,
And I can't feel at home in this world anymore.

J.R. BAXTER JR. ©1974

Study and Discussion Questions:

1. *Where did Jesus say His kingdom is from?*
2. *What are servants expected to do for their kingdom?*
3. *What is the work of an ambassador?*
4. *What gives us the right to be an ambassador for the Lord?*
5. *As strangers and pilgrims on the earth, what are our duties to our earthly rulers and governments?*

Chapter 18
MUSIC

One of the more controversial subjects that Christians discuss, or perhaps would rather not discuss, is music. Everybody loves a certain style of music. They would rather not be told that their repertoire of music is not contributing to a healthy spiritual diet, even if they know it to be true. A person's taste in music is intensely personal. We like what we like, and do not wish to change. A radical Biblicist, however, is concerned that God is pleased with every area of Christian service. This includes what they listen to, and what form of music they use to express worship.

Music is a medium of communication. Music expresses thoughts and attitudes. Music conveys emotions or tells a story.

According to human opinion, it seems the discussion never ends in trying to identify what is good or acceptable music and what is unacceptable. What music is God-honoring and what is not. Music is part emotion and causes an emotional response in the heart of the listener. Are all emotions good emotions? Music tells a story. Should all stories be told? If some types of music express lustful emotions or trigger evil thoughts, should they be enjoyed?

There are many genres of music. Rock, Pop, Country, Blues, Folk, Hymns, Gospel, Contemporary Gospel, Classical, Jazz, Big Band, Bluegrass, Soul, Appalachian, Acid Rock, Grunge, Cajun, Hip-hop and the list goes on. This is just to list some of the styles used in North America.

Some individuals declare that music is amoral, neither right nor wrong, neither good nor bad. However, songs are written by people, and people have hearts that either are bent toward sin or turned toward God. People make the harmony and create the beat. Both music and the words are created by persons with a certain goal in mind. Music is an expression of man, and every song sends some kind of a message.

So I don't like your music. You don't like my music. Neither of us believes that our music is unacceptable. We both think our music is fine but we are sure that the other's music is wrong. Who is judge? You? Me? If you, on what authority? What if I do not agree with your exposé? If it is I, how do I know that where I draw the line is the right place? Music that by my standard might be called edgy or marginal, the next person feels is fine.

The only real authority a Christian has to judge the morality of any music is the authority of God's Word. When a radical Biblicist studies the Word of God, he finds that God has a standard of holiness. He can check his music by that standard and make a determination on how it measures up.

Scripture references music very early in Bible times. The first biblical reference to music is found in Genesis 4:21.

> His brother's name was Jubal: he was the father of all such as handle the harp and organ (Genesis 4:21).

Jubal was of the lineage of Cain, and evidently he invented the first musical instruments. Music and musical instruments were used extensively in Old Testament times. Sometimes they were used for worship, to testify of the goodness of God; for example, songs were written to help remember the deliverance by God. The whole book of Psalms was meant to be sung. We find that music was also used to rally to idol worship. Songs and music were used both in worship to God and in the worship of idols.

The Bible makes it clear that Satan desires to overthrow the Christian. He will destroy people and ruin lives by whatever means is available. He has done so in the past and is continuing to use music as a tool to achieve his ends.

> Be sober, be vigilant; because your adversary the devil, as a roaring lion, walketh about, seeking whom he may devour (1Peter 5:8).

Our music (as with other pursuits we enjoy) is an extension of who we are and where we are spiritually. We do not listen to music that does not interest us, or does not resonate with our spirit. What we listen to is a window into our soul.

What we enjoy listening to is an indicator of what is in our heart. We will not enjoy God-honoring music if our heart is filled with evil. The Bible says that what comes out of the heart will be judged. Have you ever noticed how rock music, piercings, tattoos and bizarre hair styles, drugs, and immodest clothing all seem to go together? Satan will use any means to get a person's focus away from God. Music works very well to accomplish this.

The Word of God is the standard by which our music will be judged.

> The word of the LORD is right; and all his works are done in truth (Psalm 33:4).
>
> I esteem all thy precepts concerning all things to be right; and I hate every false way (Psalm 119:128).
>
> The word of the Lord endureth for ever. And this is the word which by the gospel is preached unto you (1 Peter 1:25).

God tells us that our heart's expressions will be judged.

> O generation of vipers, how can ye, being evil, speak good things? for out of the abundance of the heart the mouth speaketh. A good man out of the good treasure of the heart bringeth forth good things: and an evil man out of the evil treasure bringeth forth evil things.
>
> But I say unto you, That every idle word that men shall speak, they shall give account thereof in the day of judgment. For by thy words thou shalt be justified, and by thy words thou shalt be condemned (Matthew 12: 34-37)

Not only our words, but also our actions, will be judged. The CDs we purchase, the music we enjoy, the words we sing, are all being recorded by God and we will answer for these actions.

> We must all appear before the judgment seat of Christ; that every one may receive the things done in his body, according to that he hath done, whether it be good or bad (2 Corinthians 5:10).

How can we know if our music library is acceptable to God? The way to test music is the same way we prove every other activity in which we become involved. Hold it to the light of God's Word and test it against the perfect standard of the Holiness of God.

The problem we face concerning music isn't that God keeps us in the dark about what is good or bad music. We are the main problem in that we are unwilling to be honest. We enjoy our music. We would rather not look too deeply into what God thinks about it because we might be forced make some tough decisions. We would rather not know for sure and hope that ignorance is bliss. The scripture has a name for such actions. It is called being willfully ignorant.

1. GOD HATES IMMORALITY; THEREFORE HE HATES IMMORAL MUSIC.

> Fornication, and all uncleanness, or covetousness, let it not be once named among you, as becometh saints; neither filthiness, nor foolish talking, nor jesting, which are not convenient: but rather giving of thanks. For this ye know, that no whoremonger, nor unclean person, nor covetous man, who is an idolater, hath any inheritance in the kingdom of Christ and of God (Ephesians 5:3-5).

Immoral people write immoral music. Who else would write it? Most certainly Christians would not write it? If we immerse ourselves in the types of music that unregenerate people write and sing, we become susceptible to that type of thinking and the sins it leads to.

> Let no man deceive you with vain words: for because of these things cometh the wrath of God upon

> the children of disobedience. Be not ye therefore partakers with them. For ye were sometimes darkness, but now are ye light in the Lord: walk as children of light: (For the fruit of the Spirit is in all goodness and righteousness and truth;) proving what is acceptable unto the Lord. And have no fellowship with the unfruitful works of darkness, but rather reprove them (Ephesians 5:6-11).

2. GOD HATES UNTRUTH, THEREFORE HE HATES MUSIC THAT PROMOTES UNTRUTH.

God is a God of absolute unwavering truth, the Scripture records that God cannot lie. The following passage verifies that all liars will be punished.

> Then shall that Wicked be revealed, whom the Lord shall consume with the spirit of his mouth, and shall destroy with the brightness of his coming: even him, whose coming is after the working of Satan with all power and signs and lying wonders, and with all deceivableness of unrighteousness in them that perish; because they received not the love of the truth, that they might be saved. And for this cause God shall send them strong delusion, that they should believe a lie: that they all might be damned who believed not the truth, but had pleasure in unrighteousness (2 Thessalonians 2:8-12).

3. GOD HATES PRETENSE, THEREFORE GOD HATES MUSIC THAT IS DECEPTIVE.

In the time of the Old Testament prophet Amos, the people

were doing all the rituals that God had required of them, but in their hearts they were not right with God.

> I hate, I despise your feast days, and I will not smell in your solemn assemblies. Though ye offer me burnt offerings and your meat offerings, I will not accept them: neither will I regard the peace offerings of your fat beasts. Take thou away from me the noise of thy songs; for I will not hear the melody of thy viols. But let judgment run down as waters, and righteousness as a mighty stream (Amos 5:21).

In the New Testament we have the account of Ananias and Sapphira who agreed to pretend that they were giving to the Lord the whole price of the land they sold, but actually kept some of the money for themselves. God, Who knows all things, struck them dead for their pretense.

> But a certain man, named Ananias, with Sapphira, his wife, sold an estate, and secreted a part of the price, his wife also, being privy to it: and bringing a certain part, he laid it down at the feet of the Apostles. But Peter said, Ananias, why has Satan filled your heart, that you should attempt to impose on the Holy Spirit, and to secrete a part of the price of the land? While it remained, did it not continue yours? and when it was sold, was it not at your own disposal? Why have you admitted this thing into your heart? You have not lied to men, but to God. And Ananias, hearing these words, fell down and expired: and great fear fell on all that heard these things. Then the young men arose, and bound him up, and carrying him out, they buried him.

> After the interval of about three hours, his wife, also, not knowing what was done, came in. And Peter said to her, Tell me whether you sold the land for so much. And she said, Yes, for so much. Then Peter said to her, How is it that you have conspired together to tempt the Spirit of the Lord? Behold the feet of those who have been burying your husband are at the door, and they shall carry you out. And immediately she fell down at his feet, and expired (Acts 5:1-10).

4. GOD HATES MORAL CONFUSION; THEREFORE GOD HATES MUSIC THAT SENDS MIXED MESSAGES.

Leviticus 10 relates the account of Nadab and Abihu offering strange fire unto the Lord. God had strictly commanded them that any fire for any type of worship use was to be taken from the fire on the altar. They were disobedient and died for their sin.

The New Testament is quite clear that we cannot serve two masters. We cannot serve God and this world at the same time.

> What concord hath Christ with Belial? or what part hath he that believeth with an infidel? And what agreement hath the temple of God with idols? for ye are the temple of the living God; as God hath said, I will dwell in them, and walk in them; and I will be their God, and they shall be my people. Wherefore come out from among them, and be ye separate, saith the Lord, and touch not the unclean thing; and I will receive you, and will be a Father unto you, and ye shall be my sons and daughters, saith the Lord Almighty (2 Corinthians 6:15-18).

James puts it simply,

> Can the fig tree, my brethren, bear olive berries? either a vine, figs? so can no fountain both yield salt water and fresh (James 3:12).

The next verse states that all parts of our being (body, soul and spirit) are to come under the Lordship of Jesus Christ. Accountability will therefore be required relating to all three parts.

> The very God of peace sanctify you wholly; and I pray God your whole spirit and soul and body be preserved blameless unto the coming of our Lord Jesus Christ (1 Thessalonians 5:23).

Therefore, if we listen to music which appeals to our unsanctified nature, we can be assured that we will not be blameless before the Lord.

What type of music is approved in the New Testament?

> Be not drunk with wine, wherein is excess; but be filled with the Spirit; speaking to yourselves in psalms and hymns and spiritual songs, singing and making melody in your heart to the Lord (Ephesians 5:18-19).

We have three types of music listed in this verse with which to praise God and to edify each other.

1. Psalms - sacred songs or poems of praise, especially from the Book of Psalms in the Bible.
2. Hymns - religious songs to praise or glorify God
3. Spiritual songs - religious non-carnal music compositions

What are some types of acceptable music available to the child of God today for those who want to honor God in every area of life including his choices of music?

Following are some genres of music that fall into the broad category of being "Christian." The radical Biblicist understands that if we are attempting to have a close, meaningful walk with God, not everything that falls under the label of Christian Music will be a viable option for our listening pleasure.

Hymns: Songs of praise, worship, meditation, doctrine, and faith. It has an emphasis on the words.

Gospel Songs: Similar to hymns, but with an emphasis on personal testimony. They describe salvation, tell of experiences, and testify of relationships.

Light Gospel: More informal with an emphasis that tends to be unrealistic; nostalgia, emotion-stirring details, country life, good old days, etc. "Southern Gospel" and "Stained Glass Bluegrass" fall into the category of Light Gospel.

Chorus: A shortened version of the gospel song, with a simple and direct truth repeated frequently throughout the song. The greatest merit of the chorus is its simplicity of thought, making it readily understood by children and easy to remember.

Contemporary Christian Music: This style of music is patterned after the pop and rock music forms. This music is often romantic with little mention of sin, repentance, or the name of Jesus. Music and rhythm are much more emphasized than the message.

Contemporary Christian Music is used by many Protestant church groups to draw the un-churched to their services. It is rock music with "Christian lyrics." It becomes not a worship service, but rather an entertainment session. The Church service was never intended to be entertainment. It is not an exercise in feeding the flesh. It is a time for people to worship collectively, adoring the God of heaven and hearing words from God through the hymns and songs.

It is quite common for contemporary artists to produce religious recordings or CDs in order to make a few more dollars. We must understand that often such recordings reek of hypocrisy. The debauched lifestyles of the recording artists do not line up with the "Christian experience" they are singing about. The same goes for the Southern Gospel groups who sing relatively decent music but, as evidenced by their portraits on the CDs, the men are dressed in the latest trends and the women are dressed like fashion models. To sing songs of victory while being enslaved to the world's dress styles is hypocrisy.

Let's pick our favorite song or group and put it to the test! The purpose of this test is not to find out if you and I agree on what is acceptable to God. What we think is not nearly as important as what God thinks. God sets the standard of holiness by which we are to live. We have a bent toward sin, therefore we may not always think properly about some things. God has no such problems.

We must be honest. To be dishonest in our evaluation is to destroy the validity of this test.

1. Does the message of the song and the appearance of the group reflect the character of God?

2. To what is the song appealing? Spirit? Soul? Body?

3. Is the rhythm hidden and healthy or obvious and loud?

4. Are the lyrics clear and do they speak the truth of God?

5. Is there a light, sacrilegious approach toward the very sacred things of God? (i.e. Me and God got a good thing goin. . .)

6. Does this song give me a vision of the glory of God?

7. Does this song or singing group encourage me to holy living?

8. Does this song or group stimulate revival or a closer walk with God?

When we read a secular article or book, we critique the author and pass judgment on the truth of the subject matter. Conversely, a song with an appealing melody or beat goes right to the heart without going through all the filtering processes. We just like it. This easy acceptance increases opportunity for our enemy to slip error into our minds.

Radical Biblicists, who are concerned with truth, understand that not all music labeled as "Christian" will stand the test of music that edifies and draws us closer to God.

Study and Discussion Questions:

1. *Is music all the same?*
2. *What should music do for you?*
3. *What are the guiding principles for the believer in the choice of music?*
4. *Critique a song. How does it match up with holiness?*
5. *Is much of today's music impacting our nation for good or for evil?*

Chapter 19 RICHES

A discussion of riches, ownership, and finances can be quite divisive in the Christian church. People have widely varying opinions on the proper use of things we call our own. Books at our disposal, written by Christian authors, concerning wealth and finances do not always agree on how to handle what the Lord has given us.

On the one extreme, we have the health and wealth teachers who say that if we love and serve God, He will bless us with untold riches and good health. Directly opposing this concept are those who believe in voluntary poverty and expect that God will provide for their needs through the generosity of others. In between are many theories on what is a correct view of handling finances, resources, and possessions placed in our care.

Once again, the only safe position for the radical Biblicist is one based on New Testament teachings. There are also timeless principles found in the books of Proverbs and Ecclesiastes. Both Old and New Testament writers were well aware that riches and wealth can have a detrimental influence on our spiritual welfare, and that they are capable of drawing us away from God. King Solomon prayed this prayer, which is a good prayer for all of us:

> Remove far from me vanity and lies: give me neither poverty nor riches; feed me with food convenient for me: Lest I be full, and deny thee, and say, Who is the LORD? or lest I be poor, and steal, and take the name of my God in vain (Proverbs 30:8-9).

In Paul's first letter to Timothy he warns regarding the desire for riches:

> They that will be rich fall into temptation and a snare, and into many foolish and hurtful lusts, which drown men in destruction and perdition (1 Timothy 6:9).

Jesus when giving the parable of the Sower explained how the seed that fell among the thorns was like a man who heard the Word, but who later lost out due to the subtlety of wealth.

> He also that received seed among the thorns is he that heareth the word; and the care of this world, and the deceitfulness of riches, choke the word, and he becometh unfruitful (Matthew 13:22).

There are many guidelines and warnings the Bible has given concerning wealth. If we take these to heart, they will give insight into the way God desires us to handle the natural blessings that He has given us.

Sometimes it may seem that different passages concerning wealth contradict each other. For instance, the following two could seem to be contradictory.

(Example 1)

> Jesus beholding him loved him, and said unto him, One thing thou lackest: go thy way, sell whatsoever thou hast, and give to the poor, and thou shalt have treasure in heaven: and come, take up the cross, and follow me (Mark 10:21).

(Example 2)

> If any provide not for his own, and especially for those of his own house, he hath denied the faith, and is worse than an infidel (1 Timothy 5:8).

The two concepts set forth in these two passages may seem to be in disagreement, but they really are not. The person who has a problem of neglect in providing for his family's needs, who needs the admonition of Example 2, is not of the same mindset as the one who has hoarded money for himself and needs the counsel of Example 1.

There is warning for both. The one who loves hoarding money is as wrong in his love as the one who gets a high from spending money and has none for his family. The shoe that fits is the one we should wear.

However, if the man in Example 1 is so stingy that he will not share his wealth with his family in Example 2, then both verses apply to him.

This subject can be broken down into four main points, as follows:

1. GOD OWNS IT ALL.

God created the world and everything in it. Humans, as created beings, are part of His handiwork and are owned by Him. The universe is a closed system created by God. Man is a part of this system and cannot get out of it without supernatural help. God owns eternity past, eternity present, and eternity future. He controls the present and He owns the next life. He owns our spirits and He owns our souls. If we decide to have our bodies cremated and cast into the seven seas, God still owns them and will recall them at the resurrection.

In his sermon on Mars Hill, Paul puts it this way:

> God that made the world and all things therein, seeing that he is Lord of heaven and earth, dwelleth not in temples made with hands; neither is worshipped with men's hands, as though he needed any thing, seeing he giveth to all life, and breath, and all things; and hath made of one blood all nations of men for to dwell on all the face of the earth, and hath determined the times before appointed, and the bounds of their habitation; that they should seek the Lord, if haply they might feel after him, and find him, though he be not far from every one of us: for in him we live, and move, and have our being (Acts 17:24-28).

The psalmist says this of God:

> Every beast of the forest is mine, and the cattle upon a thousand hills. I know all the fowls of the

> mountains: and the wild beasts of the field are mine. If I were hungry, I would not tell thee: for the world is mine, and the fulness thereof (Psalm 50:10-12).

2. GOD GIVES.

We have nothing that we did not get from God, Who owns it all. Anything we are or have is a combination of elements and energy which are the building blocks of everything we know. Our bodies, our cars, our food, our furniture, our finances, are all on loan from God. We may purchase items manufactured by others using the elements that God created in the beginning of time, but they are not really ours. God has never relinquished ownership of one atom, but He does put large portions on loan to His creation.

When my wife and I married we purchased a kitchen table from a local furniture maker. We paid for it, which I suppose makes it "ours." We raised a family around this table, used it hard, had it refinished, and are still using it today 40 years later. Someday it will no longer be "ours." We have only temporary ownership. Truly, it is on loan to us. Someday we will be gone, and obviously we cannot take it with us. It may be "owned" by one of the children, "owned" by someone who purchased it at a sale, or it may be worn out and burned for firewood. If we paid $100 for it or $10,000 makes no difference, the net effect is the same, it is on loan, and we do not get to keep it.

God gives us health to work and earn wages. He gives us minds to think, tools and utensils to use, and fuel and food to consume. He gives us air to breathe and water to drink. It all comes from the hand of God. There are a number of verses which state as a matter of fact that God is the originator and sustainer of life. We have done nothing to create our existence.

> I have made the earth, and created man upon it: I, even my hands, have stretched out the heavens, and all their host have I commanded (Isaiah 45:12).

> For by Him all things were created that are in heaven and that are on earth, visible and invisible, whether thrones or dominions or principalities or powers. All things were created through Him and for Him. And He is before all things, and in Him all things consist (Colossians 1:16, 17).

3. WE MANAGE.

The wages we make and the assets we accumulate are blessings from God. We are responsible to use with wisdom those things that are entrusted into our care.

Just as a business owner would take an interest in how his employees treat his equipment or use the company credit card, God takes a deep interest in the ways His children (we who call Him Lord and Master) handle the finances and technology He has temporarily loaned to us.

The New Testament commonly uses the word steward when speaking of the responsibility we have for using the things that God has loaned us. One definition of steward is: "One who manages another's property, finances, or other affairs."

It is not hard to understand why a man who does not recognize God as the giver of all that he has, who mistakenly believes that all he possesses was gotten by his own strength and good judgment, would spend these assets on himself. After all, he is the center of his world. It is more difficult to understand why a man who claims that God is his Lord and Master, that the concerns of God are first in his life, can squander huge sums of money on himself for pride and prestige, promoting self rather than promoting the things of God and the Church of Jesus Christ.

God gives us general principles for ways we are to handle the assets He has entrusted into our care.

(A) WE ARE NOT TO HOARD OUR ASSETS.

Hoarding and selfishness are not Christian attributes. In the account of the rich fool in Luke 12, the Lord blessed the farmer with a bountiful crop. Yet he determined to keep it for himself and live a life of ease for many years. If he would have had a sharing spirit rather than a selfish spirit, he could have blessed many people. The rich fool had to give account to God for his actions and attitudes concerning the goods that God had entrusted to him.

In our childhood, most of us have had a small toy that another child wanted. We clenched it in our fist and the stronger child tried to pry it out. Both were determined to have it. Usually someone became hurt. We became angry and cried in the process of having our fingers forced open one by one. Finally, we were overpowered and had to surrender the toy.

As radical Biblicists we hold all our goods in an open hand. We allow the Lord to give into our hand and take from our hand as He will. While we have them in our hand, we use them for God's glory to the best of our ability.

We do well to stand with Job as he says:

> Naked came I out of my mother's womb, and naked shall I return thither: the LORD gave, and the LORD hath taken away; blessed be the name of the LORD (Job 1:21).

(B) WE ARE NOT TO WASTE OUR RESOURCES.

We are stewards of our natural resources, our food supply, the water, air, soil, energy, etc. We should be careful about polluting our environment. North America has become a wasteful society. Many Christians also have become lax in diligence in being good stewards. After Jesus had fed the multitude, He personally gave us an example when He directed the disciples to gather up the fragments.

> Jesus took the loaves; and when he had given thanks, he distributed to the disciples, and the disciples to them that were set down; and likewise of the fishes as much as they would. When they were filled, he said unto his disciples, Gather up the fragments that remain, that nothing be lost. Therefore they gathered them together, and filled twelve baskets with the fragments of the five barley loaves, which remained over and above unto them that had eaten (John 6:11-13).

Jesus was concerned about wasting assets even when it was a miracle and the resources were free to all who partook.

God gave man authority from the beginning of creation to have dominion over the earth. With that authority, there came responsibility.

> God said, Let us make man in our image, after our likeness: and let them have dominion over the fish of the sea, and over the fowl of the air, and over the cattle, and over all the earth, and over every creeping thing that creepeth upon the earth (Genesis 1:26).

(C) WE ARE TO SHARE WITH THE LESS FORTUNATE.

One of the marks of the radical Christian is their concern for others. They are willing to share with those in need from what God has given them. In 1539 one of the early Anabaptists, Menno Simons, wrote 17 points about what it means to have true evangelical faith. Point (4) is; it clothes the naked; (5) it feeds the hungry; (7) it shelters the destitute; (14) binds up what is wounded; (15) it heals the sick.

These are not just ideas of how a person might show his Christianity but they are proper responses to New Testament requirements. Generosity and sharing are Christian attributes.

> Charge them that are rich in this world, that they be not high-minded, nor trust in uncertain riches, but in the living God, who giveth us richly all things to enjoy; that they do good, that they be rich in good works, ready to distribute, willing to communicate; laying up in store for themselves a good foundation against the time to come, that they may lay hold on eternal life (1 Timothy 6:17-19).

Good works, driven by love for God and His people, are part of the equation that demonstrates the Christian's faith. In this way we lay up treasures in heaven. 1 John 3:17 asks a very straightforward question,

> But whoever has this world's goods, and sees his brother in need, and shuts up his heart from him, how does the love of God abide in him? (NKJV)

The love of God in our hearts causes us to do good when and where we can. We have a special obligation to those who have received salvation, and who are part of the church of Jesus Christ.

As we have therefore opportunity, let us do good unto all men, especially unto them who are of the household of faith (Galatians 6:10).

(D) DEBT IS BINDING.

Of course, the ideal financial situation is to be debt-free. However, that is not always possible, but should always be our goal. One thing we need to remember when assuming any debt is that debt is bondage. We are bound to our payments. We are under obligation to a credit card provider, a bank, or a private lender. The greater the debt we have, the stronger is the bondage and the greater is the pressure to repay. It is well documented that a major source of marital stress is related to the pressures of finances and debt.

With a loan, the lender always has the upper hand.

> The rich ruleth over the poor, and the borrower is servant to the lender (Proverbs 22:7).

The radical Christian is a man of his word and honest in his dealings. He will repay what he owes even if it takes him much longer than he had anticipated.

The pressure of over-indebtedness keeps us from enjoying the spiritual things of life, because much of what we do or think is in the context of debt pressure.

(4) SPIRITUAL CONSIDERATIONS ARE TO COME FIRST.

> Seek first the kingdom of God and His righteousness, and all these things shall be added to you. Therefore do not worry about tomorrow, for tomorrow will worry about its own things. Sufficient for the day is its own trouble (Matthew 6:33-34 NKJV).

Again, as radical Biblicists we hold all our goods in an open hand. We allow the Lord to give into our hand and take from our hand as He will. While we have them in our hand, we use them for God's glory to the best of our ability.

God does not want our riches to be the cause of our spiritual downfall. The blessings God has given us to enjoy and use for kingdom work can turn into our taskmaster. We are to use what God has given carefully and generously.

Just as Solomon, who said he did not desire riches that would take him away from God, so the Lord may not abundantly bless the radical Christian with great financial success.

Following is a hypothetical story to illustrate God's love for those who seek Him.

James, his wife, and three children love the Lord with all their hearts. They follow after and seek God every day. They are able to pay their bills, but don't have much left over. James wishes he could make more money. He would like to have some to spare for the better things in life. He would also like to give more to his church and Christian school but it never seems to be there. He is content that God knows best, and so he supports the church and home the best he can with what he has.

God loves James very much and appreciates James' servant heart. What God knows that James doesn't is that if James became wealthy, his wealth would move him away from God. It is a temptation that he would not properly handle. So, because of his sincere heart, God does not allow Satan to tempt him above what he is able to bear. In his great love for James, God withholds that which would draw him away, even though the school needs some major renovations, and James believes in his heart that he would give generously. God, knowing that James is of more value to kingdom work if he is more dependent upon God for daily living, withholds the extras. The church of Christ reaps the benefits of James remaining faithful.

Paul and his wife and four children love the Lord with all their heart. They follow after God and seek Him every day. They are able to pay their bills and seem to have plenty left over.

Paul doesn't really know why God has blessed him like He has, but keenly realizes that it all comes from God. With a servant's heart, he wants to honor God with his blessings. He quickly realizes the needs within the church and willingly and generously gives to missions and the Christian school. Paul is physically handicapped and sometimes struggles wondering why God has allowed such an experience into his life. Paul has often prayed that medical science would find a cure so he could live a normal life.

God loves Paul very much and appreciates Paul's servant heart. He blesses Paul in the area of finances because He knows that he will lay no prideful claims to it, but rather will pass it along when the needs arise. What God knows that Paul does not is if Paul were healed, he would lose his dependence on God and become proud and self-sufficient. In his love for Paul's sincere heart, God does not allow the thorn to be removed from Paul's life. He knows that Paul is more valuable to kingdom work if he is dependent on God and his fellow believers. Therefore God withholds healing and the church of Christ reaps the benefits of Paul remaining faithful.

We must realize that the tangible blessings that God has given, or the ones that we think He is withholding are only a very small part of how God works with us, His children. God knows far better than we what we really need and what is good for us spiritually. When we apply biblical principles to our finances, and ask God in faith for direction, seeking first the kingdom of God, we save ourselves a lot of grief and pressure.

We do recognize that the way we view what we have varies. Because our backgrounds and frames of reference vary, the ways that God works in each of our lives varies. Every person's situation is unique. God alone knows what we need to serve Him in the best way.

Now godliness with contentment is great gain. For we brought nothing into this world, and it is certain we can carry nothing out.

And having food and clothing, with these we shall be content. But those who desire to be rich fall into temptation and a snare, and into many foolish and harmful lusts which drown men in destruction and perdition. For the love of money is a root of all kinds of evil, for which some have strayed from the faith in their greediness, and pierced themselves through with many sorrows.

> But you, O man of God, flee these things and pursue righteousness, godliness, faith, love, patience, gentleness (1 Timothy 6:6-11 NKJV).

Study and Discussion Questions:

1. *How is it that God is owner of all?*
2. *What do you have that was not given to you?*
3. *How would a steward normally handle things entrusted into his care? List the ways.*
4. *What should be our response to God for that which He has given us?*

Chapter 20
WHY IS OBEDIENCE IMPORTANT?

New believers may question if literal obedience to the Word of God is necessary for a victorious Christian life.

Has nominal Christianity remained alive and well by living the status quo? No. The spirituality of the nominal church is in decline. In Second Thessalonians we read that before the Lord returns, Christians will fall away from the truth.

When a church compromises on the doctrines of the New Testament which are the commands of Jesus Christ, they lose the spiritual power needed to maintain a victorious Christian life. There is nothing left to save. Finally, they end up as those being described in 2 Timothy 3:5.

> Having a form of godliness, but denying the power thereof: from such turn away.

The Old Testament contains an account that gives us a look into the mind of God concerning His commandments. In Exodus God gave Moses and the Children of Israel the Ten Commandments written on stone. They were to be put into the Ark of the Covenant. This very special wooden box overlaid with gold was kept in the Holy of Holies, the most sacred part of the tabernacle. This was the focal point of the tabernacle, the center of the Hebrew worship experience. God gave Moses very precise rules relating to the method of carrying this Ark of the Covenant when the children of Israel moved from one place to another. It was to be covered with skins and to be carried by specially-appointed Levites.

After the settlement of Israel in the Promised Land the ark remained in the tabernacle at Gilgal for a season. It was then removed to Shiloh till the time of Eli, some 300 to 400 years later. First Samuel 4:1-11 relates the account of the Philistines, Israel's enemy, coming against them in battle. In losing the battle, Israel lost about 4,000 men. That night the elders decided that if they took the ark into battle, the presence of the Lord would protect His people, and they would win the victory the next day!

> The word of Samuel came to all Israel. Now Israel went out to battle against the Philistines, and encamped beside Ebenezer; and the Philistines encamped in Aphek. Then the Philistines put themselves in battle array against Israel. And when they joined battle, Israel was defeated by the Philistines, who killed about four thousand men of the army in the field.

And when the people had come into the camp, the elders of Israel said, "Why has the LORD defeated us today before the Philistines? Let us bring the ark of the covenant of the LORD from Shiloh to us, that when it comes among us it may save us from the hand of our enemies." So the people sent to Shiloh, that they might bring from there the ark of the covenant of the LORD of hosts, who dwells between the cherubim. And the two sons of Eli, Hophni and Phinehas, were there with the ark of the covenant of God. And when the ark of the covenant of the LORD came into the camp, all Israel shouted so loudly that the earth shook. Now when the Philistines heard the noise of the shout, they said, "What does the sound of this great shout in the camp of the Hebrews mean?" Then they understood that the ark of the LORD had come into the camp. So the Philistines were afraid, for they said, "God has come into the camp!" And they said, "Woe to us! For such a thing has never happened before. Woe to us! Who will deliver us from the hand of these mighty gods? These are the gods who struck the Egyptians with all the plagues in the wilderness. Be strong and conduct yourselves like men, you Philistines that you do not become servants of the Hebrews, as they have been to you. Conduct yourselves like men, and fight!"

So the Philistines fought, and Israel was defeated, and every man fled to his tent. There was a very great slaughter, and there fell of Israel thirty thousand foot

> soldiers. Also the ark of God was captured; and the two sons of Eli, Hophni and Phinehas, died (1 Samuel 4:1-11 NKJV).

Victory escaped them. The Philistines captured the ark and put it in the temple of their god, Dagon. The next morning the statue of Dagon was fallen down in front of the ark of God. The Philistines set their god back up. The next morning the statue was fallen down again and was broken in pieces.

As the ark was moved from place to place in the land of the Philistines, the people of the town wherever it rested were smitten with a plague from God and many died. Finally, after seven months it had caused so many deaths that the Philistines set it on a new ox cart and sent it back to Israel (1 Samuel 5).

From there the ark stayed in Kirjath Jearim until the time of King David. The time came when David decided the ark ought to be brought to Jerusalem, the capital of Israel. So he made plans to move the ark.

> David gathered all the choice men of Israel, thirty thousand. And David arose and went with all the people who were with him from Baale Judah to bring up from there the ark of God, whose name is called by the Name, the LORD of Hosts, who dwells between the cherubim. So they set the ark of God on a new cart, and brought it out of the house of Abinadab, which was on the hill; and Uzzah and Ahio, the sons of Abinadab, drove the new cart. And they brought it out of the house of Abinadab, which was on the hill,

> accompanying the ark of God; and Ahio went before the ark. Then David and all the house of Israel played music before the LORD on all kinds of instruments of fir wood, on harps, on stringed instruments, on tambourines, on sistrums, and on cymbals.
>
> And when they came to Nachon's threshing floor, Uzzah put out his hand to the ark of God and took hold of it, for the oxen stumbled. Then the anger of the LORD was aroused against Uzzah, and God struck him there for his error; and he died there by the ark of God. And David became angry because of the LORD'S outbreak against Uzzah; and he called the name of the place Perez Uzzah to this day. David was afraid of the LORD that day; and he said, "How can the ark of the LORD come to me?" So David would not move the ark of the LORD with him into the City of David; but David took it aside into the house of Obed-Edom the Gittite (2 Samuel 6:1-10 NKJV).

Verses 6 and 7 are the focal point of this chapter. From a casual reader's standpoint, this seems like quite a harsh punishment for a man that had a legitimate concern for the ark. Uzzah perhaps thought that the ark was going to fall off the cart and reached out his hand to steady it. This act caused him to lose his life. Did he know this was in violation of God's commands? Should not God have been pleased that the ark was being returned to its rightful place in the center of the worship experience?

This punishment by God gives us insight into the seriousness that God puts on disobedience. Four or five hundred years prior to this incident, when the ark was built, God gave Moses precise instructions on who was to carry the ark, how it was to be carried, and how it was to be covered.

> When Aaron and his sons have made an end of covering the sanctuary, and all the vessels of the sanctuary, as the camp is to set forward; after that, the sons of Kohath shall come to bear it: but they shall not touch any holy thing, lest they die. These things are the burden of the sons of Kohath in the tabernacle of the congregation (Numbers 4:15).

> At that time the LORD separated the tribe of Levi, to bear the ark of the covenant of the LORD, to stand before the LORD to minister unto him, and to bless in his name, unto this day (Deuteronomy 10:8).

> Thou shalt put the staves into the rings by the sides of the ark that the ark may be borne with them. The staves shall be in the rings of the ark: they shall not be taken from it (Exodus 25:14-15).

The ark was to be carried on the shoulders of four Levites. It was never intended that the ark be carried on an ox cart. There are a lot of improprieties between carrying the Ark of the Covenant on the shoulders of four sanctified priests and being pulled along on a cart hitched to a couple of cows.

The mindset that reasons, *It worked for the Philistines; it will work for us,* is a very dangerous one, and can lead to death. The Philistines were heathen so it did not matter if they handled the ark improperly. Even then God judged them by killing some of them with a plague because they put the Ark of the Covenant on the same level as their god Dagon.

The Israelites knew better. They had detailed instructions and were God's people. The instructions given to Moses approximately 500 years previously concerning how to carry the ark were still very much in effect.

There is a parallel here. Christians are God's people and have the New Testament to guide them. The New Testament is now approaching 2000 years old. Many Christians are pronouncing it null and void for today, but it is still very much in effect.

After the incident concerning Uzzah, David still had the desire to bring the ark home to Jerusalem, but before he tried it again he did his homework, and this is what he found:

> David called for Zadok and Abiathar the priests, and for the Levites: for Uriel, Asaiah, Joel, Shemaiah, Eliel, and Amminadab. He said to them, "You are the heads of the fathers' houses of the Levites; sanctify yourselves, you and your brethren, that you may bring up the ark of the LORD God of Israel to the place I have prepared for it. For because you did not do it the first time, the LORD our God broke out against us, because we did not consult Him about the proper order." So the priests and the Levites sanctified themselves to bring up the ark of the LORD God of Israel. And the children of the Levites bore the ark of God on their shoulders, by its poles, as Moses had commanded according to the word of the LORD (1 Chronicles 15:11-15 NKJV).

This time David had the ark moved using the method prescribed by God to Moses. It should not be surprising that all went well both physically and spiritually. God always honors obedience.

Each Christian should examine his personal life as compared to what is given in the New Testament standard. We have not yet attained. Christians have become masters at procrastinating, philosophizing, sidestepping, backpedaling, passively rebelling, and comparing ourselves among ourselves.

All God wants is wholehearted love and obedience. This is radical Christianity.

Following after God in obedience is a lifetime commitment to diligence. Satan is a master at minimizing the danger of disobedience. But God's Zero position never wavers. We must strive to make God's position our personal standard. Obedience to the precepts of God and seeking God's will for our lives is a worthy cause with far-reaching consequences. Actually, more than that, it has eternal consequences.

Our dwelling place for all eternity is dependent on our regard for and obedience to the Word of God. God has spoken. Will we believe it in faith and obey it to the best of our ability? Or ignore it to our eternal downfall?

> Henceforth there is laid up for me a crown of righteousness, which the Lord, the righteous judge, shall give me at that day: and not to me only, but unto all them also that love his appearing (2 Timothy 4:8).

Study and Discussion Questions:

1. *From Whom do we get our power?*
2. *Can we live in disobedience to the New Testament and still have the power of God?*
3. *Who tells us that obedience is not important?*
4. *Is obedience important to be received by God into His heaven?*
5. *Are you walking in obedience to all that you know?*
6. *On what basis will you be received into the presence of Jesus?*
7. *Are you ready to meet Him?*

HAVE YOU EVER WONDERED...

Where Has INTEGRITY Gone?

SCHROCK | $5.99 | 100 PAGES | PAPERBACK
ITEM# INT76082 | WITH STUDY QUESTIONS

Do you remember the time when a handshake was enough? When a man's word actually meant something? When things were safer because of the principles that governed people's lives? Have you ever found yourself wondering what happened to those days? In these tumultuous times, here is a book that touches the heart. The author, lovingly yet pointedly, calls the people of God to personal honesty and integrity.

GREAT FOR GROUP STUDIES

QUANTITY DISCOUNTS AVAILABLE

To Place an Order, Use Order Forms in the Back of this Book

A MUST READ!

What Shall THE REDEEMED Wear?

SCHROCK | $7.99 | 120 PAGES | PAPERBACK
ITEM# RED76075 | WITH STUDY QUESTIONS

Has it ever occurred to you that God may have some thoughts concerning your wardrobe? Did you ever wonder what the Bible has to say about the subject of appearance?

"What Shall the Redeemed Wear?" addresses these questions and more by looking at what the Scriptures have to say concerning this important subject.

From Genesis to Revelation and generation to generation, God calls His people to be separated unto Him. Is personal appearance excluded from that call? Can one follow the fashions of this world and still have the approval of God?

"You will find this book refreshingly honest, like a cool refreshing drink on a hot summer day. The clear, well-illustrated teaching of the old truths is a breath of fresh air for those who are seeking relief from the endless merry-go-round of fashion that has so captivated many in the Christian world."

-Glenn Yoder
Bishop, Rosewood Fellowship, Middlebury, IN

GREAT FOR GROUP STUDIES

QUANTITY DISCOUNTS AVAILABLE

To Place an Order, Use Order Forms in the Back of this Book

A Cyclorama of ENCOURAGEMENT

Then the scene shifts to Stephen, the first martyr for Christ,[1] to the conversion of Saul on the road to Damascus,[2] and to John on the Isle of Patmos.[3]

We skip across the years of the church to the Reformation, noticing the severe persecution and martyrdom of the Anabaptists,[4] and right around to our day.

Write today's date in this space ______________. This brings us near the time when the cyclorama will be full circle, when Jesus comes to bring His people home to Himself for eternity.

Right now there is a little space of grace called "today" Grace . When that space of

1. Acts 7:1–8:1
2. Acts 9:1-30
3. Revelation 1:9
4. See *The Anabaptist Story* published by Wm. B. Eerdmans, Grand Rapids, Michigan

24

"Anyone of any age will benefit from Schrock's message!"
- anonymous

SCHROCK » $4.99 » 65 PAGES » PAPERBACK » ITEM# TOW05470

When Jesus died, the Apostle Peter threw in the towel. Thinking all his hopes and dreams were blasted, he said, "I go a fishing." But Jesus rose from the dead and handed Peter's towel back. Peter got the point. After years of serving, he said, "Put on the towel of humility." After reading this book, you too will be inspired to pick up and use that towel you were ready to throw!

To order, use the order form in back of this book

IMAGINE *taking a walk with God...*

...down a winding path through fields of wildflowers, then on into the shaded forest. As you are walking, God pauses occasionally to explain the marvels of the hovering hummingbird, the flitting butterfly, the soaring eagle, the flying squirrel, or the tree frog. The conversation turns to the deep mysteries of the kingdom of God, the wonders of His love, the fullness of His wisdom, the perfection of His plan for man, and the generosity of His grace and mercy.

This is a 366 day devotional book. Each daily reading was selected from the seventh, eighth, and ninth years of the bi-monthly devotional booklets distributed free throughout the United States by Still Waters Ministry of Clarkson Kentucky. These readings are as diverse as the men who wrote them. Few books will possess so many different challenges because few books have so many authors that hold your attention.

There is a theme verse for each day and a short Bible quote at the end of each days reading. By following the Bible reading schedule for each day, you will read through the Bible in one year.

At the back of the book are the contributor's index, a Scripture index, and a subject index. These serve to enlarge the usefulness of the book.

Have you taken your walk with God today?

Beside the Still Waters
- Volume 3

$12.99 . 400 PAGES . PAPERBACK
ITEM #STI76525

- 366 Selected Readings
- One-Year Bible Reading Plan
- Written by People in the Everyday Walk of Life

TO ORDER, USE THE ORDER FORM IN THE BACK OF THIS BOOK

LEARNING FROM OTHERS...

Adam's Long Shadow

STOLL . $7.99 . 133 PAGES . PAPERBACK . ITEM# ADA76099

We learn from our mistakes. We also learn from the mistakes of others. We even learn from the mistakes of those who lived long before our time.

In *Adam's Long Shadow*, Joseph Stoll focuses on 14 men in the Bible who violated the laws of God. Studying these men can help us not to make the same mistakes that they made. Some of these men lived fruitful lives in part because of the lessons learned through failure. Others did not learn from their mistakes. Will we learn from them so that we do not follow the same paths?

TO ORDER, USE THE ORDER FORM IN THE BACK OF THIS BOOK

Order Form

To order, send this completed order form to:

Vision Publishers
P.O. Box 190 • Harrisonburg, VA 22803
Fax: 540-437-1969
E-mail: orders@vision-publishers.com
www.vision-publishers.com

______________________________ ______________
Name Date

______________________________ ______________
Mailing Address Phone

____
City State Zip

Where Has Integrity Gone? Qty. _____ x $5.99 ea. = _________

What Shall the Redeemed Wear? Qty. _____ x $7.99 ea. = _________

Don't Throw in the Towel Qty. _____ x $4.99 ea. = _________

Beside the Still Waters Vol. 3 Qty. _____ x $12.99 ea. = _________

Adam's Long Shadow Qty. _____ x $7.99 ea. = _________

(Please call for quantity discounts - 877-488-0901)

Price ___________

Virginia residents add 5% sales tax ___________

Ohio residents add applicable sales tax ___________

Shipping & handling **$4.20**

Grand Total ___________

- ❑ Check #____________
- ❑ Money Order
- ❑ Visa
- ❑ MasterCard
- ❑ Discover

All Payments in US Dollars

Name on Card ______________________________________

Card # _|_|_|_| _|_|_|_| _|_|_|_| _|_|_|_|

3-digit code from signature panel _|_|_| Exp. Date _|_|_|_|

Thank you for your order!

For a complete listing of our books request our catalog.

Bookstore inquiries welcome

Order Form

To order, send this completed order form to:

Vision Publishers
P.O. Box 190 • Harrisonburg, VA 22803
Fax: 540-437-1969
E-mail: orders@vision-publishers.com
www.vision-publishers.com

______________________________ ____________
Name Date

______________________________ ____________
Mailing Address Phone

____
City State Zip

Where Has Integrity Gone? Qty. _____ x $5.99 ea. = _________

What Shall the Redeemed Wear? Qty. _____ x $7.99 ea. = _________

Don't Throw in the Towel Qty. _____ x $4.99 ea. = _________

Adam's Long Shadow Qty. _____ x $7.99 ea. = _________

Beside the Still Waters Vol. 3 Qty. _____ x $12.99 ea. = _________

(Please call for quantity discounts - 877-488-0901)

Price ___________

Virginia residents add 5% sales tax ___________

Ohio residents add applicable sales tax ___________

Shipping & handling **$4.20**

Grand Total ___________

❑ Check #____________

❑ Money Order ❑ Visa

❑ MasterCard ❑ Discover

All Payments in US Dollars

Name on Card ______________________________

Card # _|_|_|_| _|_|_|_| _|_|_|_| _|_|_|_|

3-digit code from signature panel _|_|_| Exp. Date _|_|_|_|

Thank you for your order!

For a complete listing of our books request our catalog.

Bookstore inquiries welcome